T0144635

THE
ADVENTURE
OF PURPOSE

A journey and guide about breaking the rules,
discovering yourself, finding your purpose,
and creating a life aligned with your passions.

by
TRAVIS BARTON

This is a work of fiction. Names, characters, organizations, places, events, and incidents are either products of the author's imagination or are used fictitiously.

Copyright © 2020 Travis Barton
All rights reserved.

No part of this book may be reproduced, or stored in a retrieval system, or transmitted in any form or by any means, electronic, mechanical, photocopying, recording, or otherwise, without express written permission of the publisher.

Published by Inkshares, Inc., Oakland, California
www.inkshares.com

Edited by Brieanna Robertson
Cover design by Jessica Yaeger
Interior design by Kevin G. Summers

ISBN: 978-19-47848-76-4
e-ISBN: 978-19-47848-77-1
LCCN: 2018967131

First edition

Printed in the United States of America

This one is for the dreamers, the lost boys and girls,
for the seekers of freedom, the explorers of life,
and the pilgrims of purpose.
The road lies ahead,
and the way is within you.

INTRODUCTION

The book you hold in your hands is something I've always wanted to write—it's just not something I ever thought I'd get around to doing. See, I used to be like a lot of people in the world: I had dreams—hell, I had lots of dreams. Eventually writing a book was one of those dreams. The thing is, I never used to be the kind of guy that ever got around to living any of those dreams—that is, until I built up the courage to take the first step toward something more meaningful and learned to take charge of my life.

I guess that's where this book comes from. It's something I felt like I needed to write—not because I have a personal coaching brand and writing a book is good for business and marketing and all that jazz (none of that really matters to me, as you'll soon see in the pages of this book), but because it's a book I needed when I was growing up.

After half a year of writing what started out as a simple how-to guide, I realized the book needed to become something more—my own story of how I discovered a life of passion and purpose. One of my favorite authors, Ernest Hemingway, said, "Write drunk, edit sober," and that is the philosophy under which I wrote this book. While writing *The Adventure of*

Purpose, I did channel my own Hemingway some days—by lighting up a cigar, pouring a gin and tonic, and wearing my panama hat on my Huntington Beach balcony. The philosophy of those words influenced me the most. I spent many days and nights over the course of fourteen months coming back to this book, adding a bit more of my heart every time I came back. Some nights I would feel like I was bleeding on the page, thinking it would be too much vulnerability to share, but choosing to never edit those moments, because Hemingway might be proud, I thought.

The result of all of all of this—of a year of writing, and of thirty-four years' worth of stories—is my love letter to those in search of a more meaningful life. Storytelling is one of the earliest, and in my opinion, most inspirational means of entertainment. With that, I hope my story not only entertains you, but moves you as well . . .

Onward and upward,
TB

PART I:

THE JOURNEY

CHAPTER ONE:

The Adventure of a Lifetime

"Re-examine all that you have been told . . . dismiss that which insults your soul."
—Walt Whitman

I. Right Now—It's Your Tomorrow

I began my journey—out of a life of anxiety and depression and into a life of happiness, passion and purpose—in bumper-to-bumper traffic on a smog-filled Southern California freeway, on a morning when a voice in my head begged me to create a life I loved. I didn't know it at the time, but that was the day a simple seed was planted that would change the course of my life forever.

Still groggy from slapping the snooze button over and over again earlier in the morning, I sat in my childhood dream car, a light blue 1977 Volkswagen van, complete with a built-in bed in the back for camping trips, and Van Halen and Pink Floyd stickers on the rear window to show my favorite bands at the time. I sat in the kind of bumper-to-bumper traffic that would make even rush hour in downtown Los Angeles jealous. My brother Marcus and I—fresh out of high school and only two weeks out of a summer-long road trip of surfing up and down the Southern California coast and sleeping in the built-in bed—sat solemn and quiet, which is unusual for us individually and especially unusual when the two of us are together. This type of silent brooding is not normal for us, but in the moment, it served as a sobering reminder of the immediate contrast of two potential life paths. A life we just returned home from—one of liberating, soul-enriching, freedom-filled road trips, of surfing the best waves our Southern California coast had to offer, of being fully engaged in life, finding deep experiences; or another life, the trail that is most traveled—going to college before we really knew who we were, so we could get a job to just pay some bills, and then hopefully retiring one day with enough money to live on.

I had the morning radio playing quietly as I looked out of my driver's side window, and watched lanes and lanes of other kids our age heading to their first day of college, intermingled with middle-aged men and women driving to work, seemingly mindlessly, and very obviously dreading the day ahead. I knew they weren't all unhappy and miserable with life—they couldn't be, of course—but I certainly couldn't see anybody smiling this morning. In a moment, I saw myself in every single man and woman on the freeway. The off-ramp for our new college was the next exit and the reality of path number two was quickly becoming more and more real for me. At this sobering moment of realization, the morning surf report came on the radio. The guy at the other end of the signal was obviously excited—stoked, as surfers say, on life. He was like that every morning. Even when the waves weren't very good, he clearly loved surfing on a molecular level, and I always saw the morning surf–report guy as loving the essence of life even more. In all honestly, at that stage in my life, a bit of me wanted to be like him when I grew up—happy, carefree, perpetually stoked. I listened to "Rockin' Fig" deliver his daily morning report as I gazed longingly out of my window, watching thousands of people who, to me, appeared broken from life. These two kinds of living were so clearly and diametrically opposed in my mind—the message was loud and clear. It was a single nanosecond, a brief but profound moment of intense awakening. I got chills that ran through my entire body, my entire being.

My whole life, I was traveling down a road that I felt I was supposed to move down. I was supposed to go to school to hopefully get good grades, to hopefully get a well-paying job so I could hopefully move up the corporate ladder, so I could eventually retire with enough money to live my life. "What the hell happens in between?" I often asked myself during sleepless nights. "Am I supposed to just constantly work for some nebulous point in the future and only then enjoy my life?" I was so concerned with doing what I was told I was supposed to be doing that I never, in all my teenage years, had the time to slow down and ask myself what I should be doing. I realized that the speed at which I was moving through life never allowed me to slow down enough to discover who I was. How the hell was I supposed to know what I wanted to do with the rest of my life? A strange wave of incredible intensity overcame me. Was I going to surrender to this life I was "supposed" to be living—a life that societal expectations and cultural pressures had imposed on me? Or was I meant for a life I got to define myself, a life of joy, bliss, and happiness, the kind that "Rockin' Fig" on the radio seemed to have? I wanted to turn around, to turn my van right off the freeway and head back home. I wanted to say, "Screw it!" *Maybe I'll just become some sort of Dharma Bum or something*, I thought. But I didn't turn around, and I didn't go back home.

. . . and I was scared.

The road of expectation, the road that had been traveled before, was safe; it had a sure job with some benefits, a nice 401(k), and even some vacation time. I could live out my adventure-filled fantasies of being shaded by pine trees and soaked in high seas on the weekends, and as for my dream of traveling the world, well, that's what vacation time was for, right? My mind was doing its best to convince itself to bite the bullet and stay on track, but this uncertainty had woken up my wild but dormant heart, and on a warm sunny day on the 405 Freeway it was singing louder than it ever had before. I was always a logical person, listening to my mind and my mind only to make my choices in life, but my heart had never called so loudly before. I felt it singing. My mind was saying to keep going, but my heart seemed to ask whether this was the road that was calling to me.

At this very moment, a strange but beautiful and life-altering synchronicity happened. It was one of those moments that only happen a couple of times in life and are only ever noticed and fully recognized when your eyes and heart are open to receiving its message. I had what seemed to me to be miserable people driving on a path they had no desire to be on, horns honking incessantly and vainly to speed along the nonmoving traffic, and I had "Rockin' Fig" emphatically shouting over the radio, "It's epic out here! Five to seven feet, barreling, offshore winds in . . ."

To this day, my guess is that my mind was already made up, and I still tell myself that I just needed one small nudge. Just then I remembered that I still hadn't taken my boards out of my van from my brother's and my road trip. It was like the universe had shaken me to wake me up.

"Go," something inside me didn't say, but sang.

Is this a sign? I thought. I can't say what exactly it was, I don't know exactly what caused all these small, seemingly insignificant events to come together and create a massive shift in my being so effectively and so quickly, but I looked at my brother. We didn't say a word to each other. As the exit toward the rest of our lives was quite literally inching closer—"Time to take our exit," my mind said, but in this moment, my heart was singing much louder than my logical mind was speaking—I instead pulled left into the carpool lane. Like some sort of cosmic magic, the freeway began to open up, and so did my life.

I didn't know where this road would take me—I had no idea, and I was scared. All I knew was that I was going surfing, and something deep inside told me that this was the right decision, that it was all going to be okay. As the freeway opened up, I rolled down my windows, letting the fresh breeze run through my hair, and sang along to some Van Halen.

II. Cocktails and Dreams

Wake up! Time to get out of bed; you have a long day ahead of you. Well, maybe not just yet, you consider, as you do every single morning. Maybe hitting that snooze button is a good idea; you're definitely gonna need those extra five minutes of sleep. As every other morning, you try getting some extra rest, just a little bit of shut-eye before that damn thing reminds you again that no, it's really important to get out of bed for that routinely dreaded Monday.

This is a common theme for so many of us; it was for me, too. You're just not ready to do life today, or really any day, lately. *Just five more minutes in the solace of bed, in between my sheets where my boss can't scream at me about those "important reports" that were screwed up, and Jenny from accounting isn't gossiping about everyone at the office*—and you know, deep down, she's probably talking about you, too, on your "sick" days. And, as usual, as it has countless mornings before, the snooze button blares like a siren signaling the end of the world again before you're even able to head back to sleep for those precious five minutes. If you don't get up now, you'll be late, and last time you were late to work, you got creamed by that boss of yours. Crawl out of bed just in time to make a cup of coffee, go through the same old morning motions, and hit the road in your car that you still owe money on, only to sit in bumper-to-bumper traffic for an hour on your way to a place you absolutely dread going to. Life was so beautiful and open when you were younger. You were so happy and alive—what the hell happened?

Does this story sound familiar? I lived this exact routine for almost six years of my life and odds are that some, if not most of this story—of waking up, dreading day in and day out going to a job you despise—resonates with you on some level. Don't feel bad, though; most of us, in one form or another, are exactly at this place in life. We feel stuck, lost, depressed by an unbearable and perpetually growing sense of regret that our lives just aren't turning out the way we had always imagined they would. It's normal, actually. Most of us, in fact, are barely making it through five days of soul-crushing, menial tasks only to make it to the weekend so we can have some hope of doing something, anything, that fills us up. But usually, by the time that coveted weekend rolls around, we're too emotionally broken and too physically exhausted to do much of anything other than sit in front of the television to try to let loose a bit—never mind trying to engage in something genuinely meaningful. Certainly, this doesn't describe everyone, but it absolutely does describe a point in my own life and most of the rest of the world. Some people truly, with all their heart, enjoy this kind of life, and that's great, it is. But maybe you're feeling a bit upset at reading this; maybe it's hit you hard, and if you are upset, it may not describe you perfectly, but perhaps there's something in here that rings true. I want you to know, however, that winding up in this position isn't entirely your fault.

Even after the course-correction moment of mine on the freeway, I would often find myself in jobs that didn't call to me. I settled into all sorts of things in my life. Pressure from those around me often would make me second-guess my path in life, and I would go to work at a job I wasn't really crazy about, and more often than not, a job I detested. I knew I wasn't going toward any path that a school system could offer me, but outside of that clear decision, I was still wandering a bit aimlessly.

I found loads of fun and even a good amount of meaning, believe it or not, in tending bar in my early twenties. In fact, for the first couple of years, I loved it. I loved everything about it, from mixing up exotic cocktails and being a listening ear, having deep and meaningful conversations, to seeing some of my favorite bar patrons. One of my favorite meaningful conversations while tending bar was listening to an elderly couple tell me that they had always wanted to travel to Ireland like I had just done. Within an hour of talking with them and knocking off their excuses to not go, I got them to book the trip while still sitting at the bar, thereby pushing them into actually going. I even got really good at bartending too, doing mixology competitions to see which bartender could make the most original and tasty concoction. I even placed fourth in a flair-bartending contest—think Tom Cruise in *Cocktail*, except not nearly as '80s, but probably just as cheesy. For two years, I loved bartending, even traveling around a bit and showing my skills at different places around the country. With every place I traveled to, I contacted different bars, asking if I could come in and tend bar for a night. While I loved slinging drinks, a part of me always knew bartending wasn't what I was truly meant to do; it was only a pathway to get by for a while until I could really discover myself. After two years of slinging drinks and flipping bottles, I became jaded from the task and grew to despise it. I continued bartending for another five years, settling for it, because it paid the bills and allowed me to travel around a bit.

You see, most of us are virtually conditioned through our developmental years to dread our jobs. We're supposed to! Fun and career are two things that do not coexist in most people's minds. We are usually taught to settle for a career, to find something that will make us lots of money, or at least make us a "living"—what that means, I'm still trying to figure out—so we can earn those weeklong vacations in the Bahamas once a year, so we can buy that big house on the beach and have that fancy car that will make our friends jealous. As far as we know and as far as we can tell from our surrounding experience of what "work" is, we're supposed to sell our souls for money. We're supposed to hate going to work, because, "Hey, you're not really meant to like your job," as a high school teacher actually told me once after a career-counseling session.

Like so many people going through their youthful years of discovering themselves, that single thought stuck with me so much in my senior year of high school that I wrote it in my yearbook. "Quit dreaming," I told myself. "It's time to grow up." Man, I read that now and feel embarrassed that I ever wrote it out, but I did. Like a small, seemingly insignificant seed, that simple idea grew into something much larger for me, a giant weed that soon consumed me and became my model of the world and my future. I remember thinking, *If these are the best years of my life, what in the world do I have to look forward to?*

This single thought causes so much unnecessary anxiety in our formative years, it becomes almost unbearable to confront. When we're conditioned to think this way about our potential career, we kind of allow ourselves to settle into the path that everyone else on that proverbial highway-to-hell takes. We convince ourselves it's okay, that everyone does it, and who are we to try to do something different? We tell ourselves that this is the path that is safe and that will provide some semblance of a life, that this is the means to have some sort of freedom, to pay our bills, to make the spouse and kids happy, and to have those all-inclusive resort vacations in the Bahamas once a year. *It's better than being homeless*, we think, believing that a soul-sucking career is the only thing that's diametrically opposed to living hungry on the streets.

Let's freeze-frame here for a minute, though. Is this life of renouncing your happiness just to pay the bills a life honestly worth living? Is that torturously long morning of hitting the snooze button over and over, only to sit in traffic on your way to a job you absolutely hate, worth selling invaluable years of your life for? Why does the one joy in your weekdays have to be that iced latte on your way to work?

What if I told you it didn't have to be this way, that you didn't have to live like that? What if I told you that there was a way out? What if I told you that you can do what you love, what makes your spirit soar and your heart sing, for the rest of your life, and not just get by doing it, but make good money doing it? I'm willing to bet that if you picked up this book, you are ready for a huge shift in your life or are at least curious to explore something more meaningful for yourself. You're not alone, but you are ahead of the other billions of people by deciding to at least make the first step to beginning the search for something that deeply lights you up.

III. Taking Back Control

We tend to go through our precious years never really owning our lives. We never fully take control of our circumstances, because we don't think it's possible, or even feasible. And in surrendering control of our lives, we surrender control of our destinies. We inadvertently allow other people—family, society, bosses, and organizations—to dictate our entire existence and control our futures for us. We are amazingly comfortable with giving ourselves, our spirits, and our entire lives to the rules and expectations that others make for us. But that's the key attitude here: comfortable. Throughout life, we are slowly conditioned to settle into a life of comfort, but what nobody really tells us is that a life of comfort inevitably leads to a life of stagnation, and stagnation will always lead to a life of emotional and spiritual demise.

In her book, *Happiness at Work*, Jessica Pryce-Jones calculates that people will spend an average of 90,000 hours of their life at work, and according to a yearly Deloitte's Shift Index survey, an average of 80 percent of those people at work are unhappy with their jobs, practically selling their souls for an organization that doesn't even slightly light them up, let alone make them content. Most people are unhappy at their jobs, but stay at those jobs anyway. This is how people die before they're even six feet under. It's not that life is too short; it's that we wait too long to truly start living, if we ever start at all.

How many people do you know who seek comfort instead of what makes their heart sing? It's probable that you know someone in this position, and it's possible you're in this position yourself.

We follow that well-paved trail at one point, honestly feeling that eventually it will bring a life of fulfillment and joy. It's usually not until much farther down that trail that we wonder why we're just not feeling enriched with life. We wake up on Monday mornings with a deep sense of regret and dread. We look forward to the weekends, not ever really embracing the weekdays, not being present to the gift that they are, because we hate our jobs and just want to get the day over and done with. Forty percent of employees say their job is their biggest source of stress, so much so that according to U.K. HSE 2019 Stress Statistics, more than 15.4 million—count 'em, 15.4 million—working days are lost every single year because of stress-related illnesses. Our jobs aren't just killing our spirits; they are quite literally making us sick! This is such a phenomenon that Japan even has a word for it: *karoshi*. In Japan alone, 10,000 workers die each and every year at their desks as a result of extreme work weeks. Hell, our jobs aren't only making us sick, they're killing us!

We're told to stay at that job we hate because the benefits are good and the vacation time is nice, and, hey, that steady paycheck is pretty comfortable, too. We're told that working for an organization is safe, when the reality is that there really isn't such a thing as job security at all. To most of us, job security means working for someone else, but working for someone else is essentially leaving your career in the hands of others, no matter how well you do. How many successful people do you know who were utterly crushing it in their careers but got unexpectedly laid off? Americans, on average, have between seven to eight different jobs before the age of thirty, according to the U.S. Census Bureau! Job security as we understand it is a myth.

Time starts to pass us by, slowly at first, sure, but then it begins to move even more swiftly, almost as if to remind us of our mortality and to rub our faces in our regret. And no wonder time moves so quickly—we do the same boring, unfulfilling work, day after day, week after week, year after year, decade after decade, becoming slaves to the benefits and the steady paychecks. But what if time wasn't rubbing our faces in regret to make us feel miserable? What if it was just trying to wake us up to the facts? What if the time ticking by was just trying to tell us that we just have to make a change? We choose a life based on pre-paved trails, whether or not the scenery surrounding that trail is beautiful. I mean, we hear this path has got a stunning view if we reach the end, but ultimately, we never find it. Maybe it looked good to someone else, or maybe they were just over exaggerating, but it sure feels wrong to us. Why do we feel so lost when this is the path that seemingly everyone else is taking? Surely they can't be feeling the same way too, right? We get that job working in a cubicle, punching numbers and getting yelled at by our regional manager. We do this for eight hours a day, five days a week, because, hell, it's what everyone else does, so who are we to break off and blaze our own trails?

Society and culture say very clearly that we're to conform to their standards. And we all know what happens when we choose not to accept society's standards: we're shunned, we're made fun of, we're considered weirdos! We so desperately want to express our true selves but find it difficult to be authentic because of the immense societal pressures that surround us. If we want to fit in, we have to accept what the majority accepts and do what the majority does. We're afraid of being judged, of being different, so we stay with the herd, doing our best to impress people we don't really like in the first place. Of course, nobody dreams of working at a job they know they're going to hate. I sure didn't, and you didn't either. Nobody really has it made up in their mind that they want to spend their days selling their souls for that paycheck, but most of us end up accepting jobs we hate anyway. We do this because it's easy and it's comfortable.

But easy and comfortable never made for an extraordinary story, did they?

Sure, it's easy to go through our lives following the planned-out map, and to take that path that has already been taken—and that's exactly why most of us go down that path, because it's already been laid out for us and it's easy. It doesn't take much soul-searching or self-discovery, we just have to go with what "works," right? Some of us sincerely want to actively spend our lives journeying down the pre-blazed trail that has already been established, and hey, that's all right too. There's no judgment here if that's what really fuels you up and gets your motor running, but the big difference here is whether or not walking down that path is a conscious decision or if it is something you have just aimlessly wandered into. If you want to be a lawyer, be a lawyer, that's fantastic; we need more good lawyers in the world! If you want to work at an office and you feel like that will fill your spirit up, more power to you! For some, spending our time going down this path is a fulfilling life well-lived. The concern here is whether or not that's what you truly want in your heart, or whether it's something that's been ingrained in you. If you're walking through life solely because someone else has told you that's where you should be going, you're out of touch with who you really are. When I personally work with people, it becomes clear very quickly that most have been living a life that is in complete conflict with what their heart is begging them to do. Most people know that there just has to be more to life than the existence they've been settling for, but they're unsure of where to start.

IV. The Land of Forgotten Dreams

Viktor Frankl, an Austrian neurologist, psychiatrist, and Holocaust survivor, was the founder of a philosophical method of therapy called logotherapy. In 1946, he wrote an extraordinary, best-selling book, one of my favorites of all-time, *Man's Search for Meaning*. It tells the story of his time in a Nazi concentration camp, which, believe it or not, ultimately led him to find meaning in his life, and therefore, his reason to continue living through the horrors of the Holocaust. In his philosophy, Frankl says that man's main driving force is to discover his purpose. Now, this is largely in contrast to Sigmund Freud's popular theory, which says that all human behaviors are driven by sex and aggression. According to Viktor Frankl, man's meaning is to discover his meaning. While I would say that Freud's theory is great for surviving, Frankl's is perfect for thriving.

You have dreams, and you want to find your purpose. It's not a bold statement, because as human beings, we're all capable of really big and bold dreams. But not only are we capable of dreaming, we're also inherently pretty good at it when we get rid of all the head clutter. Like some people whom I have worked with, we have grand visions of spending our lives sailing the world, or even teaching children in Africa about sustainable living. Our hearts may be calling us to create a comic book, to play music for a living, or to shoot travel photography. It doesn't matter what it is as long it makes your heart really sing. You have something deep within you that excites you. The question is: Has it awakened in you yet?

Perhaps you fantasize daily about this dream while pretending to listen to Jenny from accounting complain about her department again, or maybe this is a dream that you've long since forgotten about. It may be that this dream was something you wanted to do when you got older, but those societal pressures broke you down until you wound up settling for the position that you're in today. Either way, there is an epic adventure in your heart just begging to be lived, but somewhere along the road of life, you've been told over and over again that your dreams are silly, that teaching children in Africa is unreasonable, that your head is way up in the clouds and you should come back to Earth with everyone else. I don't know what Earth these people are talking about—I never did figure that one out—but eventually, I realized that if coming back to Earth means being chained to a desk at an office job or having to deal with people complaining at a customer-service position in exchange for my happiness, I don't want any part of it.

Society, parents, school, businesses, politicians, and even religions are good at telling us who we should and shouldn't be—like they have any idea about who you really are in the first place. Each human being is such a complex and beautifully unique thing. We have differing emotions, feelings, likes, dislikes, and dreams, but we're forced to try to fit into the cookie-cutter life that everyone else is living. We're told what road we are supposed to travel on in life that will take us to the well-paved path, how to follow the outlines of those who came before us. Why lead our own expeditions when we can follow someone else's? It's no wonder we end up waking up from a sleepless night at fifty years old, wondering how it all got this way. All around us, society says, "Be yourself," and that's really exciting! We begin pursuing our passions and interests and maybe even an emotionally rewarding career. We get pumped about life, we feel energized, and then society comes back at us and says, "We said 'be yourself,' but not like that." It's another enigma I'm still trying to solve.

In order to truly live, to have a story worth telling your grandchildren one day, you must get out of the mindset that you will begin the journey toward your dreams, toward happiness, and toward passion "someday." Hell, "someday" always seems to be the busiest day of the week, doesn't it? But the thing about "someday" is that it never actually happens. We like to use it as an excuse to put off our dreams until everything is "just right," until the time is "just perfect," but deep down, in our heart of hearts, we know "someday" is just an excuse. You must surrender your attitude of waiting to live. Quit preparing for the perfect time to actually start the journey toward your dreams and begin living, because if you wait until "someday," you will find that someday will never actually come.

We're taught to always be preparing for some far-off part of our lives. We're never really considered to be fully here and alive in this moment, because we're constantly getting ready to finally live. From the moment we're born, we must first learn to walk, and then to speak, and then go to grade school, and then high school, and then college, and then, if we're lucky, to get a job so we can make money and buy a nice house, and then a nice car, and then to buy things we don't need, and then to work really hard to get that raise so we can buy more crap we don't really need, so we can impress people we don't really like and then save up money for retirement so we can finally start living, and then . . . (Are you exhausted yet? I am!) But by the time we get to that point, we're wondering where the hell all those precious years of life went! That's because we kept living with the "and then" mindset, constantly preparing for a "someday" that never came. But if we're always preparing and never really living, what's the point? Are you waiting to live or are you actually living?

Let's be honest here, you know this as well as anyone, you don't need to read it in a book: the true spice of life is to actually enjoy your life. If we don't enjoy our lives, I mean really enjoy our lives, why in the world are we here? Maybe you are the vice president of a Fortune 500 company, you have a beautiful vacation home in Spain, a giant yacht and enough money to make the sultan of Brunei jealous, but if you do not enjoy your time here, is it really worth it?

V. Just. Step.

Get comfortable with cultivating the mindset of history's great adventurers. There was never a direct map prior to the discovery of the ancient Ciudad Blanca ("White City") in eastern Honduras; it had to be discovered first. There had to be trailblazers to discover it. There is a widespread falsehood among career-minded people who say that you must have a well-planned and detailed outline before you take your first step into your life. This is utter nonsense and only hinders growth and stagnates life. If we stick to the paved road, nothing is ever discovered. Too often, we allow not knowing every detail about our journey to keep us from taking the first step. We're told it's dangerous to live life this way, so we think we know what we want—or at least have been told what we want—at a young age and we decide our whole lives before we know who we are. But how are we supposed to know what we want to do with the rest of our lives before we even know who we are? Make the commitment to yourself that you will figure things out as you walk along your path; life's too short to wait.

Taking your first steps with this new adventurer's mind-set will be challenging. Your learned beliefs will keep nagging inside your head, your family might verbally crucify you during dinners, your friends might even tell you to "grow up"—some of mine did; now some are asking if I'm hiring—and in the beginning, that little voice will keep on telling you that this is scary, that it's dangerous, that you should turn back. It won't be easy, but it will always be worth it.

You're going to learn some very powerful lessons along your quest. The more you test and engage yourself in your limiting ideas and beliefs, the more you will realize how you previously allowed these petty fantasies to mandate your life. You will quickly learn that your limiting beliefs do not exist out in the world—they have only ever existed within you. The more you test your learned assumptions about the world, the more you will learn to trust the direction that your heart is leading you. Like most borders of the world, where you had previously seen insurmountable walls, you will soon begin to see nothing more than imaginary lines.

Consider for a moment: What does it mean to you to go courageously and adventurously into life and how committed are you to letting your heart guide your direction? What limiting beliefs do you need to let go of in order to follow your inner compass more boldly? Chances are that you may be living with beliefs that someone else has ingrained in you. What are the people around you saying you should do with your life? Ten years from now, if you continue on the path that everyone is saying you should go down, what will happen to your spirit? Would your life be interesting? Would you love your life? Would you only be living for the weekends?

What would it look like for you to completely live on your own terms?

From this point forward, at least in between these pages, I want you to take charge and define your own life, not anyone else's vision for you—not your friends, not your family, not society, no one! This is all about you. Dream as big as you dare, as if there were no barriers between you and the life you desire, as if you knew you could not fail. Do not worry about "how" yet.

Your life purpose is your compass pointing north. Like the seventeenth-century Viking explorers searching for new lands, your purpose is like the North star, Polaris, guiding you along in this journey called life. Your purpose has been burning in you. It has been calling to you for most of your life, whether you knew it or not. And this calling, like my own, is something that you will fall in love with doing. It's something you will be wildly passionate about all while contributing to something that's much larger than yourself. Of course, it's understandable that you will be far from clear on exactly what purpose is calling to you, especially considering the pressures put upon us by the world to conform and do what others expect us to do. That's understandable; you're in the exact place most people in the world are and where I was years ago, but you must now choose to make finding your purpose your most important journey. Odds are, given the circumstances, you haven't spent much time doing any self-discovery, let alone taking the first steps on your adventure to get there. People will always say, "You'll find yourself one day." Well, you will never find yourself until you actively choose to embark on that journey. From here, we will begin to explore our hearts, chart the map to get you to your own personal Shangri-la, and embark on the greatest adventure of your life!

Are you ready?

CHAPTER TWO:

The Foundation of Transformation

"Concern yourself more with accepting responsibility than with assigning blame. Let the possibilities inspire you more than the obstacles discourage you."
—*Ralph Marston*

I. A Journal Entry Inspired by Asia

Three years after my life's literal course correction on the freeway, I felt myself lost and out of control. Yes, I knew with absolute certainty that I didn't want to settle for someone else's pre-made template of what a successful life should be, but in the years that followed I still felt aimless, and that feeling of being adrift in the world turned me into a destructively reckless person. At that point, I was more lost and alone than I had ever been in my life. Family and friends were pressuring me to move on to something more "meaningful" than my bartending job. I got offered pretty well-paying jobs at all sorts of offices and companies, but I decided to stand my ground and politely turn them down. *I'll find myself someday*, I would often think. *And when I do, it'll all be worth it.* Still, those words were hardly a comfort on most days, as I grew depressed and anxious about life.

As if that all weren't enough, I was going through the most painful heartbreak of my life, the kind of heartbreak that makes you think you'll spend the rest of your life wondering why you weren't good enough. I found out that the girl I was seeing for five years called it off with me because she was seeing someone new. But this wasn't just any old guy—of course not—it was the damn lead singer for the '80s supergroup Asia. As a classic-rock fan myself, I listened to a radio station that would often and all of a sudden play Asia. It was as if the universe were taunting me, saying, "Hey, Travis, just in case you forgot, while you're in bed crying, your ex is hooking up with a guy twenty years her senior who sang that terrible but super catchy song 'Heat of the Moment.'" I hated that song with every fiber of my being. I hated the keyboards, I hated the guitar riff, and most of all, I hated that voice. To mask the pain I was holding in, I began to drink at every chance I could. My bartending job allowed me to drink to encourage our guests to drink more—so I drank. Many times, I would even stay up all night to go surfing first thing in the morning, still with a heavy buzz from the night before.

I was on my own path, all right, just one that certainly wasn't leading anywhere good. My life's second moment of intense awakening was around this time, in my early twenties. If the moment on the freeway heading to college changed the course of my life, this moment put the wind in the sails.

By this time, I had a bit of a chip on my shoulder. I was pissed at the world, bitter that I was dealing with depression and anxiety, and I blamed everything around me for why I was miserable, alone, and flat broke. I was playing the victim card every chance I got, and I really believed that I was the victim too, that the world was just out to get me. As you can imagine, playing the perpetual victim in those years, I didn't get very far.

"Same old crap, different day," I always muttered to myself as I crawled out of bed. I know people say that kind of thing jokingly, but I really meant it back then. This was the kind of life I resigned myself to. I looked at the time on the clock—it was five, no, not five in the morning, five in the evening. I got out of bed and walked by a bottle of cabernet I had been drinking from the night before—or was it earlier this morning?—I wasn't really sure; the gin and tonics at work made my mind fuzzy before I even got home. On this particular evening, my mind wandered a bit as I walked into the bathroom to get ready for my pretty amazingly uneventful day. I considered for a moment how in the world I got to this point in my life. When I was a kid, I was so happy—full of life and dreams of living an incredibly rich existence. What exactly happened to me? When did I become so stagnant and down on my life? It had been a long process into this pit, and the heartbreak I was experiencing only threw me deeper in. When had I ever become okay with just settling and not caring? It wasn't until I got into the bathroom that evening, took a long, hard look at myself—and my entire life—in the mirror, that I decided right there to somehow, some way, change my life.

You are one hundred percent responsible for your own destiny, I thought.

I might as well have gotten this statement tattooed on my forehead in my early twenties, because when I started waking up every evening to go to work, and when I looked in the mirror and started saying that to myself, a new power that I had never felt before began to overtake my entire being. It sounds simple, sure, but it's something so many of us never learn. Hell, it took me years to fully grasp and understand this.

"You are one hundred percent responsible for your own destiny," I said to my reflection in the mirror. "Quit complaining and do something about it, you asshole." Saying it aloud had a power that simply thinking it did not. "You are one hundred percent responsible for your own destiny. Quit complaining and do something about it, you asshole." There was a weight to it this time, a very heavy one that sat in my gut. I had never journaled prior to this moment, but that morning, I felt like I had to do something substantial, something concrete. I went through my old boxes and found a red, spiral-bound notebook and wrote the following:

March 14th, 2007

For the last couple of years, I've slowly fallen into this weird pit. I don't know when or how it started to happen, but here I am, essentially at the bottom of that pit. I'm working at a job I can't stand, wallowing in my "misery" over some silly breakup, drinking too much, loving too little, giving up too early, and waking up just in time to rush out the door. I'm gaining weight and losing years. Let's be honest, dude, my life has sucked for two years. I even let "Heat of the Moment" play on the radio just to wallow in my misery, instead of changing the station. I know I can't get these two years back, I know that, but I think I can do something even better. I think I can learn from these last two years who I don't want to become. I'm rambling, I'm sure, maybe even crazy, but maybe crazy is what it takes. I believe I can learn from the experiences (or lack of) that I've had, how I want to really live, and see clearly the life I don't want to return to. I've been abusing an incredible gift, something that should be cherished. I've been abusing the gift of life, and I've been doing it by living in mediocrity—no, less than mediocrity. Complete dull, uninspired, and stagnant misery. There, I said it. But, you know what, man? I don't have to be living like this. Life is supposed to be a great adventure, one lived with passion,

at least I always said that as a kid, right? So from this day forward, I choose to not let petty circumstances, expectations stand in my way. I choose to not let this define my life, but rather to define my own life. I choose to use my challenges to bring me higher. I choose to create that life of adventure for myself. I choose to live my purpose, not someone else's, I choose to be the king of my life and live my life by my own terms.
      TB

I certainly felt on this day that I deserved an extraordinary life. We all do; I believe that with my whole heart, but I, at the time, wasn't acting like I deserved it. I wasn't earning anything other than what I was getting out of life. I was going through a midlife crisis at the age of twenty-one, and I had spent the last couple of years of my life in this crisis, focusing intently on the storm of despair I was in rather than focusing on how I could find my way out of it. Beginning to change my life was all a matter of taking my circumstances and finding new meaning in them. In Chinese, there are two characters for the word "crisis"; the first symbol means "danger," the second symbol means "opportunity." See, most of us focus our attention on the danger part of a crisis, as I was doing for my three years of misery, and this is exactly why we never grow from our challenges. Significantly fewer people focus their attention on the "opportunity" meaning of the word, and that is the reason we forever dwell on our problems instead of finding a way out or figuring out how to grow from them. It's all a matter of seeing things through a new lens. It's never our circumstances that define us; it's how we choose to respond to those circumstances.

See, the thing is, I wanted an extraordinary life, but I also realized that nobody owed it to me either. If I wanted to be happy, nobody was going to give me that happiness. If I wanted to discover my purpose, nobody was going to do it for me. If I wanted to be wealthy, nobody was going to hand me a million dollars. Nobody was coming to save me from myself, and you know what? It wasn't their responsibility to help me; it was my own responsibility! "Nobody owes me anything," I remember proclaiming into the mirror. And in deciding that, I gained all the power I would ever need. In taking responsibility for my destiny, I began to openly see the abundance and opportunity in my life. A smile crept onto my face—the first real, honest one I'd had in months. That small, simple mindset shift had such a huge impact on me. It changed my life: I was ready.

II. Quitting the Blame Game

It took me a very long time to understand that nobody but me was responsible for how my life was going to turn out, that I was the sole person responsible for my destiny. I desperately needed to understand something that I now consider the greatest lesson of my life: When it comes down to it, when everything's said and done, society, the school system, my parents, my job, and everything else never controlled me. They have never controlled my or your past and they certainly do not control our future. But I gave them power to control my life by doing nothing to change my circumstances, and, of course, that didn't get me very far.

The person you grew up to be and the person you will become was not created by the circumstances you've been dealt; but the person you are today is created by how you choose to respond to those very life circumstances. This single shift in mindset and attitude has made all the difference in my life and will make all the difference in yours. You and you alone—not anyone else you may want to blame—are the biggest hurdle that is preventing you from living the life that is waiting to be lived. While societal pressures may condition us to live a certain way, society is not to blame here—you are! If you want anything to change in your life, whether it's a big or a small change, you must take the power back and change it yourself. The world only has the power to dictate your destiny if you allow it to hold that power. The most powerful thing I've discovered is that you manifest your destiny.

Yeah, that's right . . . let that sink in for a bit. It's a completely radical concept and mindset shift in a culture of complaining, but it's appropriate. Most people sit around in the same spots their whole lives, waiting for something, anything, to save them from themselves. They wait for some external force, person, or stroke of luck to shape their lives. And then when nothing extraordinary happens, they usually blame the entire world, everyone but themselves, for where they're at in life. These are the kinds of people who will always come up with excuses for why they're not successful, why they're not happy, or why their spouse is so horrible. And it probably wouldn't surprise you to hear that, according to them, it's never their fault. There is absolutely nothing they could have done to help themselves; the world is out to get them and they're just too helpless. You will never hear someone with a true success story—no matter how you define success—complain about how the world was out to get them. Even if someone else were to blame, you will never hear a person living on purpose blame others for the position they're at in life. Even if they were dealt a horrible hand in life, they will take responsibility for learning how to play it well!

We see the blame game everywhere we go. It's far too easy to place the blame on someone or something else when things go wrong in our lives. "Someone else must be responsible for me hating my job, for me being overweight, for me being unhappy! Someone else must be responsible for this mess, 'cause it sure ain't me!" But no matter how poor your place in life seems to you, placing blame is akin to placing complete control of your life into someone else's lap. Stop and think for a moment about how scary and helpless that prospect is. When we blame others for all that has happened to us, we are also giving them the power to dictate our own futures. If where we ended up today were the world's responsibility, it would be the world's responsibility where we end up in our futures. When we blame the world for the paths we have taken, we are literally holding other people responsible for our futures. Not only that, but blame brings helplessness and depression into our lives; taking responsibility facilitates growth and empowerment.

Life, for so many of us, is much easier when we're just being the victim. When it's always someone else's fault that you haven't succeeded or that you're unhappy, it's not your fault, and if it's not your fault, then you've done everything you can, right? Wrong! So wrong.

I'm about to give you all the power you can ask for—the power to influence and take charge of your life in a single sentence. A sentence that I want you to write on your mind forever. A sentence that fueled my own adventure of purpose and those of hundreds of others whom I've worked with. Are you ready?

You are 100 percent responsible for your own destiny.

Life isn't about what happens to us; it's all about how we choose to respond to what happens to us. We are all responsible for our own lives, successes, happiness, health, and futures. When we place blame on others for our misfortunes, we are also giving others control of our fortunes. When you place responsibility on yourself, you are giving yourself an incredible power to actually do something to turn your misfortunes into fortunes. You can wish that things will get better your whole life and then die in vain, never seeing results. Wishing is like playing the lottery—how many people ever win? Sure, you can wish for a better future, but you can actually ensure one by working for it.

This work all starts with our mindset. If we begin to take responsibility for our lives instead of blaming others, we will take action to remedy our situations and direction. When we are responsible, we don't want to let ourselves down, not even for a minute, because that means having to face ourselves in the mirror tomorrow morning knowing we didn't do anything to change our situations. We can't complain, because we know we have the power to do something about it. When we are responsible, we can't blame others—not our parents, our teachers, or society. We know we are in charge of our futures . . .

. . . and that gives us all the power in the world to make all the difference in our worlds.

CHAPTER THREE:

Creating Happiness

"This planet has—or rather had—a problem, which was this: most of the people living on it were unhappy for pretty much of the time. Many solutions were suggested for this problem, but most of these were largely concerned with the movements of small green pieces of paper, which is odd because on the whole it wasn't the small green pieces of paper that were unhappy."
—*Douglas Adams*

We each have something in common with every single person in the world, and that commonality is that we all want to be happy—every single one of us. Happiness is a feeling that we all crave, and we know deep down that when we finally achieve it, we'll have finally made it in life. But the trouble is that not many of us are really sure how to achieve it or if it's even something we can achieve.

Starting out on my journey to find happiness in my life, I wasn't sure that it was something that was possible to attain. We've all heard the phrase "the pursuit of happiness," but sadly, most of us don't really know how to pursue happiness, because most of us don't know where the road that leads to happiness is. As children, we are inherently happy; it's routinely not until later in life that happiness escapes us. Sometime between our adolescent and our adult years, we get the notion that working toward happiness is impractical and even selfish. Being happy, however, isn't a selfish act—it's actually one of the most selfless things we can do. Happiness doesn't just enrich our lives but also helps enrich the lives of everyone else in the world as well. When you're happier, you make the people around you happier, and you're in a sharpened mental space within which to explore your purpose in life.

Of course, living a life of purpose and being engaged in what makes you come alive would make anyone happy, but this is backward thinking. Happiness comes as a result of living our purpose, yes, but the foundations of it must be practiced first, so that we are in a clearer and more positive headspace on our journey. An attitude of happiness develops a mentality not only of positivity, but possibility as well. This is the outlook that makes living richly and finding our lives' purpose that much easier . . . and certainly more fun.

From my teenage years all the way to that moment of reclaiming my power in my early twenties, the keys to happiness always seemed to elude me. And I'm not talking contentment here, as I was already a very joyful kid growing up; I'm talking about full-blown awakening—nirvana, ecstasy. I was utterly convinced that living a joyful life depended on extrinsic things and outward circumstances, something that perhaps only the wealthy elite had, and maybe a few Tibetan monks hidden away deep in a cave at the top of some snowy peak. Perhaps there was just something in the Himalayan air? For all I knew, there might as well have been. I couldn't afford to climb a mystical Himalayan mountain to ask for the answers from an old monk. I certainly wouldn't call myself wealthy. And of course, to my disappointment, happiness was never taught in school. I wanted to find happiness; at this point in my life, I was actually ready for it. I wanted it more than I wanted anything, but how was I going to find this happiness?

After taking responsibility for my life in my early twenties, I set off on my own personal journey of discovering what it means to live joyously—maybe to find happiness, but probably to come back empty-handed, I had guessed. I read a lot about mindfulness; I studied books and lectures from the Dalai Lama; I learned tons about the Eastern philosophies as presented by Alan Watts, specifically one of his most famous and (what I would consider) most beautiful works, aptly titled *The Book*. I asked young and elderly people about what happiness meant to them, and at one point in my darkest days, I began to ask myself. After enough reading and talking about it, maybe understanding it on a philosophical and even neurological level, I knew that happiness wasn't something to be passively learned—it was something to be actively experienced. I quickly figured out that happiness didn't seem to be something that would come to me in a book or in a lecture hall. It would have to be something that I inwardly acquainted myself with if I were to ever truly understand it. That's when I dug up my old passport—which at the time only had one Mexican stamp from a weeklong trip down to Cabo San Lucas some years prior—and I began to travel, I mean really travel. Every single stamp that I would secure in that passport soon came with stories, new philosophies, exciting ideas, and nostalgic memories of self-discovery. Through these wanderings, I talked to innumerable people, gathering clues that would ultimately lead to discovering my own happiness and even eventually, my own purpose. Like an explorer searching for the answers of an ancient mystery, I began my journey with a single step, or rather, a single plane ride down south to Central America, and a few years later, I discovered that I never really had to go very far at all to find those keys to happiness.

No matter where I went in the world, no matter whom I talked to, over time, I learned that happiness wasn't this elusive external thing waiting to be found. It was, in fact, an outlook anyone could cultivate. I found some of the happiest people in the world who had nothing in the way of possessions, and I found some of the happiest people in the world who had abundance. Happiness, it seemed, was something internal. Happiness, true bliss, and awakening were already in me and had been my entire life; the tinder was only waiting to be sparked so the fire could burn on. My travels and my engagements with the world taught me that a happy life is, in fact, within all of us. I had been carrying it with me the whole time . . . and so have you.

Learning that true happiness was not the same as contentment was a massive turning point in my understanding of bliss. And learning that happiness wasn't an ambiguous thing to be found, but rather an art to be practiced, was the catalyst that led me to living life on my terms, lighting my heart with passion, and discovering my life's purpose. Yes, I found that the prerequisite to purpose is finding your happiness, not the other way around. This discovery will be the same for you as well. Call it joy, bliss, euphoria, whatever you want, but know that it's a state we're searching for, not a tangible thing. And just like anything we practice, like learning to speak a new language or play an instrument, when we keep doing it for a consistent amount of time, we tend to get pretty good at it. Trying to discover your life's purpose without first cultivating a happy and positive mind is like hitting the gas pedal on your car—pedal to the metal—while still having your hand brake pulled up. You may have some leverage, you may sputter along, but you will never get where you want to go. Imagine what would happen the moment you decide to let off the brake, with the gas going full throttle. You're flying at incredible speeds to your destination . . . your purpose. In this book, you will learn to pull down the hand brake.

In the last century alone, only an average of 1 percent of articles published on psychology have been about happiness. The other 99 percent have been about the negative side of psychology, discussing topics like anxiety and depression. Actually studying happiness is a bit of a new concept, but something that has been sorely lacking in the psychological field until now. In the last decade or so, there have been countless books written on the subject and even more charlatans who try to sell you their crazy "happy pills." It's a jungle out there, but I'm going to share with you what I learned through my travels around the world about how to cultivate your own happiness within—a way to implement three philosophies that you can take with you immediately to begin creating long-lasting joy in your own life and thus putting you in the right headspace for embarking on your discovery of purpose. While it's great to know about what creates a happy existence, the key principle here is to actually implement this knowledge into your life, to embody these ideas as I did throughout my travels. These aren't all the elements of a happy life—some others will be scattered in the pages of this book, to be explored and discovered. I'm sure there are even more elements that I haven't uncovered on my journey of life, but these are the three that create the foundations.

I. Nicaragua

As inspirational-maxim writer William Arthur Ward said, "Gratitude can transform common days into thanksgivings, turn routine jobs into joy, and change ordinary opportunities into blessings." And he could not have been more spot-on, as I discovered while traveling in Central America—my first stop on my quest to uncover the secrets of happiness. I'll never, for the rest of my life, forget traveling to Nicaragua on a surf trip with a good friend of mine. This was my first big trip out of the United States other than Mexico years prior. Sure, Mexico was fun; having cocktails on a white-sand beach, bodysurfing in clear, crystal-blue water, and seeing one of my musical idols, Sammy Hagar—the second lead singer for the greatest American rock band of all time, Van Halen—front row at his tiny cantina, was the pinnacle of my teenage years. But this time, I was a little older—though not particularly any wiser—and I wasn't seeking tequila and rock and roll; I was seeking answers (and maybe even some great waves all to myself).

My good friend John was coming along with me on this trip. He was an infinitely better surfer than I was, so besides learning about what it takes to become happy, I was almost equally excited to learn a thing or two about becoming a masterful surfer. We boarded our flight to Nicaragua at 12:30 a.m. and I spent the entire flight there staring out the airplane window, wondering what was waiting for me in this far-off land. Was it happiness? I didn't know, but at least I knew the surf forecast was off the charts, and that was a hell of a start. John and I departed on a red-eye, and only hours later, we watched the sun rise over the water as a new landscape began to emerge. It was a profoundly poetic thought: crossing over into a new day, I was greeted by a new country as well. I was a little child seeing a new part of town for the first time. As any traveler will tell you, there's something truly special about a first trip, something so exciting that will make even the most hardened man giddy with anticipation.

We landed and I got my coveted second stamp in my passport. *The second of many more in my life*, I promised myself as we stopped to grab our bags. John and I emerged out of the airport into a sultry humid air that felt like there was a hole blown into the ozone layer right above us. This atmosphere was something entirely new to me. The heat and stickiness was everything you would imagine from a tropical country; I loved it. We left the Managua airport, packing our surfboards and bags into the bed of a pickup truck that was there to carry us to our destination at Playa San Diego, where we would have good waves all to ourselves. The air was sweltering. I was exhausted, but I was smiling.

Through the smiles, joking around, and talk of how good the surf would be, I took almost immediate notice of the poverty all around me—locals pleading for money at every stop, shells of once-thriving storefronts on the side of the road, and beat-up cars sputtering along a two-lane road. My eyes were opened for the first time in a long time. Through this brief experience, I began to comprehend how fortunate I was—to have been born in a place and time where I didn't need to worry about where my next meal would come from, or to even have a place to call home. I wasn't ten minutes out of the airport before I saw something—a single moment in time that would forever change my outlook on life.

As I looked out of the window, through the children washing the window of the pickup truck in hopes of receiving even the smallest amount of spare change, I noticed scores and scores of tents on the side of the road, in between all the shops and hubbub on the Managua streets. These tents, I soon realized, were essentially small makeshift villages that people were living in. On closer inspection, I realized that they really weren't tents at all. What I was seeing were entire families living under pieces of tarp hung up on trees and poles. This was home to them. My first real impression of Nicaragua outside of the incredible heat and humidity was seeing entire families crammed into small, makeshift tarp homes in parks on the side of the road. *Surviving*, I thought, *but not really living*. The smile I wore was very quickly consumed by sadness and pity.

But then I saw something else, something so profound I began to question everything I was ever taught about being happy. I saw a little Nicaraguan boy. I never learned his name, I don't know how old he was—although I could guess about eight or nine—and I never learned his story. This particular boy was shirtless, wearing nothing but soccer shorts that looked a little too small for him. He was barefoot, and he was playing with nothing more than a plastic grocery bag. At a stop, I watched briefly as he used this plastic grocery bag as a makeshift kite. He carried it in the wind, allowing the bag to open up and fly a few feet before picking it back up and doing it again. Now, seeing this small child playing with nothing more than a plastic bag, I became immediately heartbroken. I felt sorry for him—no clothes to wear, no house to live in, and no real toys to play with, just a piece of someone else's trash to try to find some enjoyment in. *Every child should have toys to play with*, I thought. I remembered getting a Ninja Turtle with the wrong color mask for my birthday once. I remember throwing a small tantrum because it wasn't the right color, and in that moment, I felt shame in how disappointed I was in opening it up. It was obvious to me that this kid would have been thrilled to have a Ninja Turtle to play with, no matter what color mask it was wearing. I wanted to help him, but I either didn't know how or was too afraid to stop the car and ask.

Through my guilt and pity, though, a funny thing happened. As we passed this boy, I could now get a view of his face. I expected to see sadness, but what I saw was entirely unexpected; he carried with him the biggest smile I had just about ever seen. In that single second, my life dramatically changed again, as my perspective on happiness began to shift. In that moment, I was confused, I was shocked. As we continued to drive out of the city and into the countryside, this Nicaraguan boy on the side of the road never escaped my thoughts. I thought of an interesting contrast between this little boy—who was virtually homeless, lived in poverty, and had nothing, but was utterly and completely happy—and all of the people I knew back home who were wealthy and had everything—nice homes and cars, all the money you could ever ask for—but were utterly miserable. I asked myself, *Why? What does this boy have that made him so happy that others do not?*

It wasn't until our third day, when we were all alone, surfing some once-in-a-lifetime, epic waves, that I gained some clarity. I sat in the tropical Nicaraguan water, saw a giant wave position itself right in front of me, heading right where I was sitting. I didn't have to paddle much to catch it. I dropped in and chose to go right, sliding down the steep face of the wave, my heart beating through my chest. As I made the steep drop, the wave began to curl over my head, crashing over me. I was in a surfer's paradise, inside the barrel, the eye of the wave. I shot out, heard a giant hoot from John, as I shouted across the water that this wave had to be at least twelve feet tall (although surfers are known to highly exaggerate their surfing stories, and I'm not going to say I'm better than any of them). After pulling out of this wave, something clicked about this little Nicaraguan boy. Maybe I needed that moment of exhilarating passion to see it all clearly; I don't claim to know for sure. But what I do know is that I was, in that moment, in a state that was open to receiving the answer that was right in front of me my whole life.

I paddled back out toward John after what had been the wave of my life, sat next to my friend, and said, "There's a lot to be grateful for here, brother."

See, in my days of reflection, the answer culminated on that single ride. I believe that the answer—what this boy had that so many of us do not, what he had that was more valuable than all the riches in the world—was gratitude. It was the ability, learned or not, to be thankful for the things that he already had in his life. The deep lesson I learned in the Central American Pacific Ocean was that maybe happiness comes from our ability to focus on wanting what we already have in our lives rather than focusing on having what we want.

This thought reminded me of the principles of Zen Buddhism, which I had read about earlier that year, and particularly the concept of "the middle way." Buddha said that the right perspective to find peace is to find the middle way between excess and self-denial, meaning that we must embrace spiritualism as well as materialism. This is a stark contrast to what I was used to, surrounded by those either focused solely on material wealth or on spiritual wealth. There was a balance, and whether this boy from three days ago knew it consciously or not, I believe he had it.

Coming to this realization and keeping the middle way in my mind was the beginning of my experience in practicing daily gratitude. You see, the happiest people on this planet appreciate the things they already have in their lives. Do you have your health? How lucky you are, how fortunate you are to be alive, to breathe this air another day! I get to go home from wherever I am in the world and have drinkable water straight from the faucet. Most of us take even that for granted, but imagine how many people go thirsty because they have only filthy water to drink! Maybe you don't like your job much—something we will, of course, work through in these pages—but think of all the people in the world who have to fight every single day for food because they have no job at all.

Simply giving daily gratitude is not enough, however. It's important to find deep and profound gratitude, as this is the first and most crucial step to attaining deep and profound happiness in life! Outside of a spiritual practice, in psychology research, giving thanks is greatly correlated with immense happiness. Don't just say you're grateful, though; everyone does this and it never really amounts to much. In many American families, a big tradition before Thanksgiving dinner is to go around the table, expressing what everyone is thankful for. Often, these are half-hearted words we say quickly just to get down to eating the turkey and stuffing. We usually just say we're thankful for our health and family and get on with it, no big deal. Of course, those are two of the most important things we can be grateful for—but ask yourself why you're grateful for these things. Really reflect on what it means for you to have a healthy, beating heart and good mental stability. On top of the usual health and family, I always like to reflect on something a little extra. Ask yourself what else you're grateful for and get really into it.

What would happen in your life if you started practicing gratitude every single day? I know the answer, but I want you to explore and discover it for yourself. When you choose to practice giving gratitude—not just during the holidays, as most of us do, habitually practicing it every single day, and often—I'll tell you from personal practice, it's pretty difficult, if not impossible, to have a sour day (or even life, for that matter) after reflecting on such positivity in a consistent way.

If you ask John about our trip to Nicaragua, the first story he might tell you is how I screamed after thinking I was being attacked by a bull shark, only to find it was my foot touching the reef. But the story I always tell is how I learned about true gratitude. After a week of surfing our brains out and a couple of nights of drinking enough Flor De Caña con Piña to make a pirate proud, I returned home from Nicaragua and made practicing daily gratitude a habit in my life. Once I chose to commit to practicing gratitude, an incredible thing happened: I became much happier—perhaps not quite on the level of a monk living in a Himalayan mountain cave, and certainly, I didn't think, to the level that this boy from Nicaragua had achieved—but for the first time in my life, I felt like I was on my way.

II. Japan

A little over a year later, the itch to leave the United States was again heavy in me. The minute I returned home from Nicaragua, before I had even unpacked my bags, I dreamed of where my next trip would be. I immersed myself in all sorts of travelogue writings, from Paul Theroux's *Dark Star Safari* to Ernest Hemingway's *A Moveable Feast*. I even learned Spanish, and a bit of German, so I could become a better traveler and connect with locals around the world. Travel began to consume my entire being. I traveled to Ireland for St. Patrick's Day; trekked all across the United States, getting lost in the swamps of New Orleans, surfing rivers in Montana; and even returned back to Nicaragua for more surfing.

By the time I was considering my next trip, I had hung a giant map of the world in my living room. The thing covered my entire wall, just over my couch, as a constant reminder that there was a whole world to see, and I had only seen a small fraction of it. It was well after midnight, and I sat on my couch reading about the wanderlust-fuelled travels of Anthony Bourdain. The itch was strong, and I wanted to book a trip before I could talk myself out of it the next morning. I knew by then that I could convince myself I just couldn't afford it, that the place I was working would not let me have the time off and that everyone around me would convince me not to go. There was a part of me that was excited about doing something that others would call stupid, but that I knew would reclaim a fire in me. After all, I seemed to be on a mission, breaking the rules of normal and beginning to blaze my own path. Plus I didn't want to read about Anthony Bourdain traveling the world anymore; I wanted to actually do as he did—I wanted to travel! I wanted to test the limits of what others would think was stupid, so I decided to, right in that moment. Without much hesitation, I finished the last of my Guinness, stood up, pulled a dart out of the dartboard that my roommates and I played on, stood in the kitchen about twenty feet away, and threw the dart at the map. Wherever this dart landed, I was traveling to.

I don't know if it was a sign, but the universe, or at least the dart, told me exactly where I was going next. The world was the target, and Japan was the bull's-eye. The land of the rising sun was calling and now, in my mind, there was no turning back. (Well, technically, it didn't land on Japan, it landed on the Sea of Japan, but I sure wasn't going on a cruise.) I sat on the couch and booked my trip immediately. I was going to stay in the Tokyo district of Shinjuku. Japan! So steeped in culture and mystery to me. I knew nothing about Japan; I didn't know the culture, outside of being raised on the Godzilla films as a kid, and I certainly didn't know the language, but I had four months to learn as much as I could and immerse myself in the culture.

I got off my flight early enough on a March morning to explore Shinjuku before I could check myself in to my hotel later that afternoon. I wandered the streets and explored downtown Tokyo. For the first time in my life, I was taken aback and awestruck by something that was man-made. The brightly illuminated neon lights in the foreign streets, the Buddhist temples that lay between sex shops and noodle bars, the cleanliness of the sidewalks without a single trash can in sight, and of course, the Golden Gai bars, which is a web of six tight alleyways that hold over two hundred minuscule, shanty-style bars. I was culture-shocked, and I loved every ounce of it. I reveled in not being able to speak to the locals or to read the signs written in Kanji. Being lost was kind of fun, and I was learning. and with no itinerary and no plans, I felt free.

It wasn't until a very fast and full week into my Japanese adventure that I managed to finally build the courage to work through the complicated train systems there and leave Tokyo for the city of Kyoto. The transportation was jarring to me, as I couldn't for the life of me read the signs on the exits. I had to match the signs on the exits with what I saw on the map. Japanese Kanji, I discovered, was not so easy to learn. I didn't want to look like a tourist in Japan, but I certainly looked like a tourist in Japan. Holding a map to my face, disoriented and adrift in a sea of people, the only thing that was missing was a fanny pack to complete the evolution to full-blown tourist. I found it a much more difficult experience than I had expected, but I also found it was kind of fun. I felt like a real traveler now, no matter how I might have looked to the locals. *Ernest Hemingway*, I thought, *might even be proud.* Three and a half hours later, I matched the sign on the train with the one on my map. I stepped off the train and into the very quiet and picturesque city of Kyoto.

Within no more than ten minutes, I became lost once again, this time not surrounded by towering neon skyscrapers and seedy sex shops, but by small-scale storefronts and temples. Wandering the streets, I tried to match my map with the signs on the road unsuccessfully. I stopped in to a few shops to ask for help, but just like in Tokyo, nobody could speak any English to help me. Of course, I didn't really expect them to either, since I was in their country and I hadn't learned their language. To get my bearings again, I tried to locate the train station that I arrived from, but couldn't even manage to do that.

I was roaming aimlessly in a foreign country, halfway across the world. Another half hour flew by when I decided to stop into a sushi bar to get something to eat and try to recalibrate. I quickly made friends with three Japanese men at the bar. They were laughing because when I ordered sake, the waitress was slightly confused. She seemed to ask me something, but of course I couldn't understand anything she was saying. She returned with a glass of tequila. *Not what I ordered*, I thought. Through the confusion, I learned that *sake* in Japanese simply means "booze." I was ordering booze like some sort of crazy, drunk American, not the rice liquor I was hoping for. The three men came to sit next to me, laughing the whole time—not at me, it seemed, but with me. As they sat, they ordered a round of sake for us all. We couldn't speak to one another outside of hand gestures, but we became fast friends. They ordered us another round of hot sake and squid guts. I obliged, of course, as I learned it's rude to turn down gifts in Japan, and hell, who am I to let my cultural tendencies interfere with theirs? After two rounds of sake, I began to feel pretty good about life, and even practiced giving gratitude for being lost in such a beautiful country with such friendly people.

I left the sushi bar and quickly came across a small shop of Japanese trinkets. In this shop, I saw a small bowl that struck me, as it was exceptionally beautiful, and learned about the ancient Japanese philosophy and art of Kintsukuroi, or the art of repairing pottery.

No, I didn't learn how to repair pottery in Japan—bear with me. To the Japanese, it is not enough to just repair pottery and make it look brand new, like it's never been broken before. In the art of Kintsukuroi, the idea is for the blemishes and cracks to be illuminated rather than hidden. The understanding here is that the piece is even more beautiful after it has been broken; therefore, the Japanese repair their broken pottery with gold or silver lacquer to make these cracks and breaks flourish—to make you say, "Wow!"

The eventual finished piece, of course, is nothing short of beautiful. If you've never seen a broken bowl lacquered with gold, it is truly something special—so special, in fact, that many Japanese craftsmen in the late fifteenth century deliberately shattered pottery so that they could repair it. But to me and many others, the philosophy of the art is far more beautiful. Showcasing the cracks in a "broken" bowl or cup with gold and silver is a metaphor that all things, even bad, are simply a normal part of life, so rather than giving up, life is made even more beautiful by finding the gold lining within.

See, at this particular time in my life, I was in a position that almost sent me into a second downward spiral of misery. It seemed to me at that point that absolutely nothing was going right for me again. If anything, it all seemed to be going pretty wrong and, the worst part is, I knew I was responsible! I was still lost in life, unsure of where I was headed. I had lost my job of three years, and I was flat broke. It struck me as funny how such a small bowl of pottery had such a massive impact on me that day in Kyoto. I began to think of my life and my downward spiral in the spirit of Kintsukuroi. I realized how I had easily spent this time in my life feeling sorry for myself and as a result, perpetuating even more sadness and misery.

I purchased the bowl, of course, left the shop, and began to walk around Kyoto a bit more, and just then, it started snowing. The streets were soon covered in a stunning snowfall and the cherry blossoms around me became decorated in white. The Buddhist temples held a certain otherworldly beauty in contrast with the lush natural surroundings. I felt a bit of a tingle. Was this a sign of some sort? I didn't know, but I chose to take it as one. *Signs*, I thought, *hadn't failed me yet.*

Lost on the side streets of Kyoto, unable to find my way back to the train station, I committed myself to bringing the philosophy of Kintsukuroi into my life right then and there. I chose to view my challenges with a new perspective. Instead of focusing on how horrible my situation was, I began to focus on the silver lining, the opportunity in my situation. I chose to focus on what was good, like the gold that lined the broken parts of a bowl repaired with Kintsukuroi. In the time it took to take a breath, I decided to shift my mindset, and a funny thing happened, I began to see opportunity for growth and even some happiness. I saw opportunities that I would have been completely blind to if I had chosen to keep dwelling on my shattered pieces. I found a beautiful perspective: Because I didn't have a job, I now had time to begin my dream career. I was broke, sure, but I also had no debt, and that allowed me to travel. *That is something most Americans can't claim*, I thought. I found a new perspective that, because I was lost in Japan, hell, I was lost in Japan, baby!

So, sure, you can throw your proverbial teapot away because it was shattered and broken in the past. Or you can make your teapot shine brighter than ever before. Just like those fifteenth-century Japanese craftsmen who purposefully broke their ceramics to repair them using Kintsukuroi, you don't have to just deal with your past pain, but you can actually be proud of it, shining and becoming more beautiful as a result of having been broken. You can actually be happy that it happened! That day in Japan, I learned that not only is it my choice to take responsibility in my life, but it is my choice to find positive perspective in life's many challenges.

Show off your scars, let them shine like gold lining a pot; learn from your pain, allow it to be seen like silver and gold holding together a shattered bowl. Become a better person as a result from all the damage that has been done to you in your past and all the challenges you are facing using the philosophy of Kintsukuroi. There is a natural rhythm to life that is largely out of our control. We cannot master our circumstances; we can try, but that is not how the world works—it will never bend to our will. But we can learn how to master the way we think about these circumstances, and that will make all the difference.

This exercise, of course, is a little more difficult to implement in your life than giving gratitude, but it is one that, if practiced—the key word here is "practice"—can create some incredible results. Gratitude can be easy because it is focusing on the good in life, but perspective can be hard because it makes us see the good in the bad. If something really bad happens—some event that is painful, or an encounter with someone who has greatly hurt you—do not dwell on how horrible the situation is if you want to be truly happy.

That's right, I can hear you now—easier said than done, right? Yes, exactly! That's why these are practices, and why this one especially takes some effort. Instead of focusing all your energy on the problem, on the hurt, on the broken pieces of your proverbial pottery, focus on what opportunity you can gain from this experience, no matter how horrible you think it is. Focus on what you can learn; focus on how you can grow as a result. Find perspective in life's inevitable misfortunes and you may be surprised at how you can grow from them!

Late into that night, I finally found my way back to the train station and made it back to Tokyo, safe in my hotel bed. My new bowl lay on the desk next to me. I fell asleep, not stressed, not anxious about my place in life and who I was. I was smiling . . . I wasn't sure what life had in store for me, but I felt content in the present moment and excited for what lay ahead of me.

On my flight home, armed with my new mindset of giving profound daily gratitude and finding positive perspectives in life's challenges, I sensed a subtle newness within me. I was becoming a man of possibility and positivity. My life's direction began to open more vividly in front of me. I was not only seeing opportunity in my future, but also finding joy in my present. I didn't sleep the entire thirteen-hour flight home. I was too excited, too happy about the gold that lined my life.

III. Denmark

"We leave in a week. You're coming. Pack your bags!" my good friend Megan told me, in a phone call that lasted no longer than a minute.

I practically salivated at the adventure of it all. Megan was doing a couple of workshops in Norway and Denmark with her business and invited me to tag along with her so she could have some positive company along the way. The thing was, she hadn't given me much notice beforehand. I had less than a couple of weeks to pick up some bartending shifts so I could gather the funds and commit to going to Scandinavia with her. While a year prior, this trip was something I would have convinced myself I could in no way do, I had become the type of man who reveled in getting out of his comfort zone and committing to things others would say he was crazy for committing to. Throwing a dart at a map and booking a spontaneous trip to Japan was a testament to breaking societal norms and living to tell the tale. I practically reveled in the fact that this offer came on such short notice. I thought it would make a great story in my book, if I ever decided to write one. A couple of short weeks after this offer, and after many double shifts of slinging drinks behind the bar, I was on a plane to Norway—the land of the midnight sun—to hike in their woods, cross off a bucket-list item by seeing the legendary fjords, and then, head to Denmark and maybe learn a bit about happiness from the place that economics researchers from around the globe deemed one of "the happiest countries on earth." How could I not be excited?

Norway was as spectacular as you often hear it is. Untapped wilderness and beautiful people, not to mention the legends of trolls and fairies abundant in Norwegian folklore, something I had been fascinated with in my youth. We even ran into a giant troll statue in the middle of the woods on a hike, just to make it clear to us that we were in fact in Norway.

But it wasn't until I arrived in Copenhagen, Denmark, that my happiness mission began to enter my mind again. Walking through the city, I immediately felt its vigor and vitality. What was once a Viking fishing village in the tenth century now had stunning architecture on the water and some of the best food trucks I've ever visited. These two things instantly made Copenhagen one of my favorite cities on this planet, but what really struck me, almost immediately, was how kind and generous everyone was. Everyone said "thank you," people smiled at you for no reason other than to spread a little love, and locals passing by started friendly conversations with complete strangers. At the time I didn't know much about Denmark, but I did know I was falling madly in love with it.

We spent a day in the capitol, and in the evening headed three hours out of the city into a town called Aarhus to stay at a hostel for the next two days. As I soon learned, this hostel was located right next to Marselisborg Palace, the summer residence of the Danish Royal Family, and adjacent to the palace was a vast park. This park was rich and vibrant with green lawns, brilliant works of art, stunning ponds, and towering trees that all connected the coast of the bay. The best part of this arrangement was that the park was open to the public while the queen and royal family weren't home.

They weren't home.

Megan and I checked into our hostel, threw our bags into our room without unpacking, and decided to scope the place out a bit. As I sat in the lobby, taking in the experience while having a cup of black coffee, a friendly man walked up and introduced himself to me. His name was Brian, and we got to talking about all sorts of things, from the history of the queen's palace, to our shared love of soccer and the possibility of our respective countries qualifying for the next World Cup, to my inquiries of whether Scandinavians really believed that trolls and fairies exist (to which I sadly never got a clear answer, but that leads me to believe that Scandinavians are generally intelligent people—so why would they believe in something like that unless there were evidence to support it? I digress).

We shared a couple of cups of coffee, as I was still fighting a bit of jet lag, and we had the kind of conversation you have with someone whom you've known for years, the kind of conversation usually reserved for late-night bonfires at the beach, gazing at the stars, and asking the big questions in life. I love these kinds of conversations; I could have them all day. After some time, I finally got around to asking him about the long, cold winters in Denmark and how they dealt with eighteen hours of straight darkness every year for an entire season.

"Do you take supplements? Do you have sun beds? What do you do to deal with the constant darkness during your winters?"

His answer, like everything else on my journey to discover how to achieve happiness, was painfully simple, yet beautifully profound: "Smile," he laughed.

His confidence in the answer led me to believe that he was onto something, but I probed curiously. He went on to tell me, over another cup of coffee, about the power of smiling.

"There's the fact that happiness makes us smile, of course it does, but smiling will also make us happy."

This is one of the quirkiest and most out-there concepts that I learned on my travels. Upon hearing about this in a Danish hostel, I was as skeptical as anyone would be, but I did remember that I was in one of the "happiest countries on earth," so I listened with wide-open ears. (After all, Scandinavians tend to be very smart.) He went on to tell me about the scientific studies that have shown how smiling, even when we're sad and down, oftentimes makes us happy. I was so interested in this concept that when I arrived at my bunk that night, I looked it all up only to be not-so-surprised that Brian was spot-on.

He told me about the long, dark winters in Denmark and how he and many other residents of his country chose—in one form or another, though not exactly in the way that I had learned—to give some gratitude and find a positive perspective. He told me how he in particular would choose to smile even when he didn't necessarily feel like it, and especially in the winter. If you feel down, I learned, one of the best things you can do for yourself is to force a smile. Upon doing my research, I discovered that smiling, even when you are sad, releases dopamine, which is basically the natural feel-good drug. So while for the first few seconds of smiling you may feel pretty silly—as I did, sitting in this Danish hostel with a man I just met—soon you start to become happier, like really, genuinely happier! Does it sound funny? Sure, it does. Does it work? Absolutely, it does! You'll start thinking happy thoughts, even when happy thoughts are the last thing on your mind, and that will perpetuate more happiness throughout your day. Just like Vietnamese monk and Zen master Thich Nhat Hanh said, "Sometimes your joy is the source of your smile, but sometimes your smile can be the source of your joy." Who was I to argue with a Zen monk, or even with a resident of one of the happiest countries in the world?

Try it yourself: fake a smile! Do it right now. Forcing yourself to smile—even when you're really, really down—after only a few seconds begins to give way to a genuine smile, that wrinkly-eyed kind of smile, and ultimately, some pretty authentic happiness. This isn't nonsense either—it's backed by real, honest-to-goodness science. When you force yourself to smile, your facial muscles are tricking your brain into releasing the kind of neurotransmitters that really help you become happy. I'm sure the last thing most of us want to do when we're feeling down in the dumps is to put on some sort of goofy, fake smile, but try it right now and see what happens.

But Brian wasn't done with me quite yet. The last thing he told me was that smiling in itself is not enough. "You must give a smile to others too!" he said. "To make other people happy is happiness." This was something I understood right away. A simple philosophy, like everything else I learned on my journey, was right in front of my face the whole time. Like Yoda mentoring Luke Skywalker, with a simple, brief statement, this man had made a huge impact on my life. To give happiness, and to do it unconditionally, I discovered, was a key in unlocking happiness within myself. This simple-to-understand concept, in fact, formulated much of the direction I chose to take my life in thereafter.

Over my years, I've learned that discovering and living a life of purpose tends to come pretty naturally when we stop focusing so much on what we can do for ourselves, and instead focus on what we can do for others. Part of discovering your own true north is to uncover who you can give your gift to, and then to do it selflessly. This is a head start in the right direction. An attitude of complete service, I discovered once I started coaching, leads to prosperity.

Brian and I parted ways. Megan and I then took the opportunity to wander around the forests, visit the bay, and walk around the queen's palace. We wandered the forest for a bit and I remember the sun shining just perfectly through the trees. Small slivers of light made their way brightly through the branches of the three-century-old beech trees above us. I began to feel a sense of contentment and peace sweep over me. (The beauty I felt in this moment is difficult to express, but that forest is a place I urge you to experience for yourself.) I sat on a tree stump of no particular importance in these woods and closed my eyes. I soaked in the natural artistry all around me, until my reflection of the beauty of this country turned into a reflection of the beauty of life itself. I thought of my place in the world, of my discovery. It all overwhelmed me and I began to well up with tears. I wasn't just happy; I was, for the first time in my life, on this tree stump in these Danish woods, profoundly and deeply happy. I was euphoric. I was fully absorbed, present in this moment, and honestly alive.

While, as we will soon explore, there surely is a sense of happiness in pursuit, profound and long-lasting happiness doesn't come from out there—it comes from inquiry within. Happiness, I realized, is the way in which you travel, not the destination to which you arrive. Happiness, true and honest happiness, is not out there. It can be learned out there, as I learned it, but it lies within us all, waiting to be lit. Through my travels, I discovered that happiness is the mindset you choose in the face of what happens to you. Some things are just out of our control, and that's all right. We can't control the world—nor should we—but we can control how happy we choose to be. It's our choice to find gratitude, to find perspective, and to smile. It is our choice to actively pursue happiness in our lives, not only to bring about a better present for our lives and others but to lay the foundations for a better future.

IV. GPS

While sitting on this tree stump in Denmark, I realized the three keys to happiness that I had experienced in the world: gratitude, perspective, and smiling. Again, like anything profound I had ever learned, it was painfully obvious and right in front of me the whole time:

Gratitude

Perspective

Smiling

Or: GPS.

So, when you find yourself stuck, sad, lost, or even depressed, when you can't seem to find the road to get back on track—that elusive road to happiness—you don't need to climb a mystical peak in the Himalayas and ask a monk how to achieve happiness; you don't need to have a six- or seven-figure income. You just have to remember to follow your own GPS.

Finding authentic happiness and lining our minds up with these teachings are essential parts of living passionately and purposefully. It can be difficult, if not near impossible, to discover what you're put here in this world to do if you cannot first become happy. Choosing and practicing happiness is like making the first steps on your quest of purpose.

CHAPTER FOUR:

Pura Vida

"All grown-ups were once children . . . but only few of them remember it."
—*Antoine de Saint-Exupéry,* The Little Prince

I. Too Much Guaro and Some Tasty Waves

Through all of my travels, I had yet to go anywhere out of the country with my brother, Marcus, and that was something I felt needed to happen. Life is too short and the bond between us had always been unbreakably strong. We were born to have adventures together, but in the past, it had been challenging to find the time. We had talked about traveling to Costa Rica together for a number of years, but never really found the means to make it happen. We would plan to go one year and then finances would get in the way. We'd plan again the following year and then the timing just wasn't right. This went on and on until we finally made the commitment, brother to brother: "No matter what, hell or high water, we're going to Costa Rica this year!"

So we went to Costa Rica that year.

Our first adventure together was to a little town called Puerto Viejo de Talamanca, on the Caribbean side of the Costa Rican coast. Like traveling to Nicaragua, what started off as a surf trip to catch the most powerful wave in the Caribbean, Salsa Brava, soon turned into something much more. Together, we both learned the spirit that has stuck with us through the years, the spirit of *pura vida*. *Ticos* (native Costa Ricans) have been using this phrase for the better part of five decades, and it's pretty much the law of the land out there, but it was something we wanted to know more about after hearing it at every stop during our first day wandering the town. We heard it as a greeting, as a goodbye, and even as a substitute for "awesome!" The translation of pura vida is simple but has a much deeper meaning to the people of Costa Rica. In English, the phrase translates to "pure life," but as I learned cliff diving off a giant rock in the middle of the Caribbean Sea, these words are not enough to describe the true spirit of pura vida.

Marcus and I decided that rather than getting a hotel on our travels, we were both going to sleep in hammocks in the middle of the rainforest. The first night was fruitlessly spent trying to get some sleep in the middle of a rainstorm. Of course, there's nothing quite like Caribbean rain, so it was difficult to get more than a few minutes of sleep without the loud thunder waking us up. Sleep just wasn't in the cards on our first night, I realized, and then, even through all that rain and thunder, we heard the distant sound of drums being played deep in the forest. Rhythmic bongos, *djembes*, and congas all seemed to be playing in rhythm with the natural sounds of the storm. The pulsating sounds of rain, thunder, and drums were accompanied by loud and excited shouts. Lying in that hammock, not knowing where these jungle beats were coming from, I imagined tribespeople were having an ancient ceremony; it certainly sounded like it. It was a bit spooky, but our interest got the best of us. We got out of our makeshift beds and started walking, very timidly, toward the source of the sound. Eventually, we came to discover an authentic Costa Rican jungle party going on in the middle of the night, in the middle of forest, in the middle of the storm, right by the beach. We were astounded. What seemed to be the host of the gathering stumbled and danced over to us and offered us some homemade *guaro*. Now, when traveling to Costa Rica, my word of warning is to be wary of drinking too much guaro, as it is the local drink infamous for a soft bark, but a nasty bite. One guaro turned into two, and two into three. A phrase we learned in Costa Rica is that one guaro is not enough, and two is too many.

The jungle party had locals and travelers playing pulsing drums together throughout the night, keeping the dancing going and the rain gods in playful spirits. I managed to get the group to slide around headfirst on our bellies through the mud, kind of like a natural slip 'n' slide. As the hours drew closer to sunrise, dozens of us found our guaro-influenced selves running into the sea, swimming around in a reef shelf in a storm that I had never seen anything like. You could say that the guaro had something to do with that; but I say that the magic of Costa Rica and the spirit of pura vida was already creeping into my being. We spent the rest of the night being pummeled by rain, telling stories with locals and fellow travelers in a reef shelf. If life was a party, we were the ones dancing.

On our second day, my brother and I woke up a bit late into the morning. My hangover and fuzzy memory of the previous night suggested we'd had a hell of a welcoming to the country. Of course, too much guaro led to us waking up with the feel-good effects of the drink long gone only to be replaced by the price of a pulsing skull and not being able to recollect much of the previous night. Having such an otherworldly hangover, we chose to rejuvenate a bit and take a walk to a place down the dirt road for some tacos. Upon arriving at Tasty Waves, we met an American expat named Bryton who owned the place. We got to talking about his business, why he moved to Costa Rica, and what he loved about the Costa Rican life-style. It didn't take long for Bryton to learn that we were both new to the country and ignorant of the pura vida lifestyle. On being enlightened to this, he asked us to come back to Tasty Waves in an hour. "Bring something to swim in," he said. We didn't know what he was up to, but we both agreed without hesitation. How could we not?

We met back up with Bryton an hour later, right outside his Tasty Waves cantina, which now looked to us to be closed. A sloth up in the trees greeted us as Bryton walked out and let us know that he shut his doors so he could take us on a bit of an adventure. *Something like this*, I thought, *would never happen back home, ever!* Closing a restaurant to take a couple of gringos you've never met before on an adventure? Of course, this seemed like a very welcoming thing to do, but never back home. I laughed to myself.

We spent close to twenty minutes hiking through the dense rainforest of Puerto Viejo until we arrived on the beach. The sun was beating down on us. The sounds of woodpeckers tap-ping on trees and the soft waves crashing on the shore were our soundtrack. Our new guide pointed his finger out to the sea. My eyes followed his gesture to a giant rock sitting alone in the Caribbean Sea, which looked to be about a twenty-minute swim. With nothing else, Bryton said, "Just follow me," jumped into the sea, and began to swim for it. Of course, with little-to-no hesitation and with no coaxing, as we were in the market for a decent-sized adventure, we both decided to follow. I won't lie, the thought of bull sharks looking for a quick bite out of a couple of gringos entered my mind more than once during our swim. It was almost as if I were convinced a bull shark had actually tried to attack me in Nicaragua, as though he'd spent a couple of years plotting his revenge and had now followed me to Costa Rica. In fact, it was on my mind the entire time, but I'm happy to say we made it safely in one piece, if not very tired, to the lonely rock standing tall in the sea. The size of it was much larger than it looked from the shore; it seemed to be about forty feet tall.

Bryton—an American by birth, but clearly a local to Costa Rica—skillfully and effortlessly climbed barefoot to the top of the rock in no more than a handful of swift movements. The two of us followed with significantly less fluent style. As we finally summited, Bryton began to tell us about Costa Rican life and the spirit of the *ticos*. He explained to us why he left America to start his own quaint cantina in the Costa Rican rainforest, and the importance of living life like you mean it. As we all sat together on the rock, looking out into the vast and mysterious sea, we talked about what it takes to be truly happy in this life and shared a couple of adventure and drinking stories. We were fast friends. I marveled at the surrounding untapped beauty; from this vantage point, man's conquest of nature had yet to take hold.

Curiously, through our many stories and unrelenting laughter, I asked what exactly "pura vida" meant. We had heard the phrase over and over during our day and a half in town, and we wanted to know the meaning. Bryton took a brief pause, looking out into the Caribbean Sea and then back to the tropical rainforest. With his eyes turned toward the mainland, he said, "Life is good, man. You gotta go and enjoy it. You gotta play." And as if to express the spirit more than the words, he jumped off the forty-foot cliff face and into the crystal blue water. I thought I understood. I followed. "Pura vida!" I shouted, a bit like a free and uninhibited child as I made the leap after him.

We spent the afternoon jumping wildly into the sea, with the sun shining warmly on our backs.

Pura vida—we got to talking about it on our way back to Tasty Waves. It means a lot of things to a lot of people. But the way I embraced it, and how I kept the spirit of it alive in me after that day, was by thinking that life really is rich and good; it's just up to us to explore that. As the spirit of play seemed to follow with the words pura vida during the rest of that afternoon, leaping from that cliff in the middle of the sea, and for the rest of our time in Costa Rica, it is in that spirit that I see the meaning of those words.

II. "Children Are My Spirit Animal"

There is the attitude of pura vida, an inner spirit of play, inside every one of us, anxious to be set free. It's so funny—when children are born into this great big world, they instinctively tap into this beautiful gift called creativity by boldly unleashing their playful spirit. Typically, as we grow older, we are apt to sacrifice our inner spirits of play in order to make way for what society deems the "important things" in life. Rather than being engaged in what we truly want to do, we start giving up on our passions and what makes us come alive in order to spend more time at the office, to please the in-laws, and to be more engaged with what society tells us we should be doing. We tame our inner wild things, and the true sadness is that we usually do this unconsciously, at the mercy of the world. Our inner wild things remain unsatiated, inwardly reminding us every now and then—all too often during midlife crises—of their desire to be fed. We give in to what others expect us to be, bending our lives to others' influences, and in doing so, we cut off the line that our hearts are speaking through. At this point, we don't listen to our hearts because we can't.

Do you remember what it was like to be a child? Do you remember what it felt like back when innocence was still in your heart, back when you didn't have a care in the world other than what you were going to do with your friends after school? Remember when you had such incredible vision and absolute belief in yourself? When you 110-percent knew that you could accomplish anything? As a young boy, Batman inspired my first dream to become a detective—and then I wanted to be the president of the United States, and then an astronaut exploring the cosmos—all before I decided I wanted to guide people out of their limits and into a life of passion and purpose.

When we were children, we were completely wild, we felt free, and sure, maybe we were a little cocky, too, but baby, we sure dreamed big! We were engaged fully in life; we followed our interests no matter how silly they seemed, and with no concern given to anyone who thought we may be "weird" or "offbeat." Our decisions as children were based purely on our hearts, and that's because our hearts were open and completely wild. We embraced pura vida one way or another when we were kids. I had a good friend, Ryan Heflin, who told me during a late-night beach bonfire while camping and playing music together that "kids are my spirit animal." He meant that children were free from the pressures of day-to-day life, truly free to be themselves because they hadn't been beaten by society's expectations yet. That really hit home for me. What a great thing: to aspire to be like a child.

We all have that inherent pura vida quality of a childlike mentality; we are born with it. It is a part of all of our essences and souls. It is not until later, usually as we enter school, that we are slowly conditioned that our dreams aren't really possible. It doesn't happen all at once, of course, and none of us is actively doing it on purpose, I believe, but over time, we are subconsciously held back from the life we aspire to live. The first step to embarking on the adventure of a lifetime and of living your dreams is to find that child within you and fearlessly and wildly follow your own heart—not someone else's pre-made template. Some things were meant to be tamed, but you weren't one of them.

This complete belief in yourself that you held as a child was true, too! It isn't until we grow a little older that we become conditioned by the world and by ongoing disparagement of ourselves and our abilities, and we start to believe that achieving so much is just too difficult or too far-off to actually reach. By the time we reach our teenage years, we're often jaded, but maybe still a bit hopeful. By the time we reach adulthood, we're often bitter shells of our youthful, hopeful, and happy glory, having been instilled with fear and doubt throughout our lives. We didn't learn how to stop believing in ourselves until we grew up.

Kids create enthusiastically, playfully, and without inhibition. Kids will make a game out of anything; they will see the joy in what grown-ups see as boring and trivial; they will see a challenge as a great adventure to be overcome. Like my nephew, kids will make one of the most fun games out of a couple of building blocks and a pillow. They don't need anything over-the-top to have fun, don't need more to create; they create the fun themselves.

Who do you think has life more figured out?

Kids tap into their creativity like it's second nature, because creativity is natural. We all have it; most of us have just forgotten how to tap into it as we've grown older. How did we lose that? We lose that childhood spirit of creativity and play by assuming identities that social and cultural expectations put upon us, and we are taught to constantly play defense in life. But playing defense in life and living playfully are two mutually exclusive things. Pretty quickly we begin to show up in the world, not from a place of creativity and play, but from a place of fear and panic. Play cultivates creativity; creativity helps to solve problems and to fully embrace life's challenges.

Our model of the world quickly becomes based on fear, and because of that, we begin to make unfulfilling decisions. We get tired and jaded, and as a result, that powerful and important inner child slowly fades away. In the beginning of our coaching relationship, I always hear clients say, "I can't," or "I don't know how!" They hire me as their coach because they think I'll give them some sort of magic answer that will change their lives. But I don't need to do that because I only need to unleash the inner child within them and tap into that spirited creativity. When people say, "I can't," or, "I don't know how," I don't believe any of that for a second. Those are just excuses. Somewhere in there, in your heart of hearts, you know perfectly well how, you know perfectly well that you can. It's just a matter of tearing down that fear-based attitude that society has led you to believe is the right attitude, and of unleashing that pura vida, that inner child of creativity. Because a child is so creative and playful that they will always learn how to do it or find a way to make it work.

Your heart may have been silent lately—maybe for a year, maybe even for decades—but deep down, if you listen, you'll notice that it's calling you toward something extraordinary, and the more you let your pura vida spirit run free, the more emphatically your heart will communicate to you what it wants. When you unleash your spirit of play for long enough, your heart won't just speak, but it will sing, baby, and it will sing so loud that you won't be able to go anywhere other than where it is begging you to travel. You must find your inner wild thing; unleash it and let it run free before you even find your true purpose. If cultivating happiness begins your first steps, unleashing your spirit of play opens your eyes so you can see your passions and life more clearly.

To live with pura vida, at least to me, means to let your playful side run free, to pursue a life of active engagement in your interests and passions, without the expectation of getting anything out of it other than enjoying it in the moment. It means to be engaged for the sake of being engaged—for the fun of it all. It means pursued immersion in what makes you come alive, not just waiting and hoping that it will come to you. Wander into what fires you up; jump off the proverbial Costa Rican cliff and into the sea of life, but don't expect to find purpose there—don't expect to get anything out of it other than what it is. If you've been sitting in the same place in life, working at the same job, living with the same standards, and not playing outside of that, you have forgotten the thrill of being a child. Just to be engaged in it with the spirit of play is to open your eyes to your limits and your purpose.

III. The Beautiful Game

On our fourth day, Marcus and I rented a couple of bikes from Puerto Viejo's town convenience store to try to explore the surrounding forests a bit more. We hopped on and began pedaling toward a destination unknown—not sure where we would end up but confident that the journey would lead us somewhere spectacular, somewhere new and uncharted to us. *"¡Hola! ¿Qué tal?"* I would shout from my bike to the people walking the streets as we rode aimlessly along dirt roads. I had spent the three months prior to our trip learning enough Spanish to be able to have a conversation with the locals. My trip to Japan, while teaching me about profound happiness, also taught me how important it is to be able to speak with the locals. I was conversational and very proud of it, speaking

Spanish and interpreting for Marcus at every chance I could get—even when it wasn't necessary—just to do it.

If a turn in the road looked interesting, we took it; if a place looked enchanting, we stopped to take it in; if someone looked friendly, I spoke with them. We were infected with the pura vida spirit and made this day all about unleashing our inner children. On one particular turn off the main road and up a steep hill, we met a group of four boys who looked no older than ten or eleven. We stopped the bikes and I asked them, "*¿Hola, cómo estás? ¿Qué hay de divertido por aquí?*" which roughly translates to, "What's fun to do around here?"

"Ah, *bienvenido a Costa Rica. Síguenos,*" one boy responded.

"What did he say?" Marcus asked.

"He said to follow him," I replied.

"What do you think?" Marcus asked.

I thought briefly. "Well, I think we should go!" I said as I got back on my bike and followed behind these kids.

Pura vida, I thought.

We followed our new friends up the side of a seemingly endless hill, growing more and more exhausted as we biked along. Thirty minutes passed before the four boys walked into the jungle, beckoning us to follow.

"*Síguenos,*" a couple of them repeated in unison.

By this point, we had to walk our bikes as the ground turned into soft, thick mud. Slowly and carefully through low tree branches, we maneuvered ourselves to keep up with our new guides. After ten long, uncertain minutes through the forest, the four boys turned around together. This was the moment of truth. We had spent close to forty-five minutes wondering in the back of our minds what our fate was going to be. Maybe naively following four strange kids we didn't know into the middle of a foreign country's rainforest was the first stupid decision I made in my long streak of stupid decisions that would finally have consequences.

"Bienvenido a Costa Rica," one welcomed us as he moved aside a veil of leaves. What he revealed took my breath away.

A mammoth waterfall sat just beyond the veil of leaves, flowing fiercely down into a small lagoon. I watched a brightly colored toucan fly by and into the tropical trees that surrounded our view. It was stunning and nothing short of epic.

"Pura vida!" the lead boy shouted as he jumped into the water.

I glanced at my brother, and we both shouted, "Pura vida, baby!" as we followed our new friend's lead. We spent the entire afternoon swimming in that secluded lagoon, diving around and shouting like small children, fully immersed in a moment that we knew we would remember for the rest of our lives. We climbed the rocks, stood proudly next to this massive waterfall, and jumped off the cliffs, laughing in good spirits for hours.

"¿Juegas fútbol?" one child asked me as we all lay in the mud, resting from our afternoon-long swim in the forest. He was asking us to play soccer. Now, my brother and I are both rabid soccer fans, so accepting an invite to join in on a game with locals was a no-brainer for both of us.

"Por supuesto," I affirmed excitedly, *"¡vamos a jugar!"* We were going to play the beautiful game of soccer with some locals in another country—something I had always wanted to do since I fell in love with the game as a little boy.

The rest of the afternoon was spent kicking a soccer ball back and forth in the Costa Rican rainforest with four ten- and eleven-year-olds who might as well have been professionals, as far as we were concerned. They moved around us effortlessly. If we weren't having so much raw and uninhibited fun, we might have been humbled. Every goal that either team scored came with shouts of "pura vida!" and slides in the grass to celebrate—and maybe even showboat a little.

This is what life is all about, I kept thinking to myself. I was having one of the most incredible experiences of my life, all because I embraced the spirit of pura vida and decided to make a spontaneous decision to play. I could have easily allowed some unfounded fear of the unknown dictate my decision, but as listening to my heart has never failed me—from the moment I started listening to it on the 405 Freeway, to every time I've booked spur-of-the-moment trips—I chose to listen to my heart on this trip as well. If I kept making decisions in my life based on unfounded fears, I would never have any semblance of an extraordinary life, let alone any extraordinary experiences. No, I chose to experience this trip in the essence of pura vida and on that trip, I chose to take that spirit home with me as well. This choice has made all the difference between dreaming of an extraordinary life and actually living one.

IV. Growing Old—Never Up

We will grow old and there's not a thing we can do about it. As we move along our journey of life, we grow old and up, taking on more responsibilities and more obligations, getting married, and paying bills. We have kids of our own and learn what it means to be a functioning member of society—an adult! Slowly, we become stale over the countless days of waking up, hitting that snooze button, and working hard to try to take care of ourselves. It is usually during this time in our lives that we get so caught up in where we think we need to be going that we completely lose sight of what it means to really be alive, only dreaming of days that could be spent jumping out of bed, ready to tackle the gift of a brand new day.

There's no way to head back to where we came from, and every single day we move closer to the end of the road. That inevitable finish line looms ahead as a reminder that life is only a momentary trip, a gift. This sobering truth can be a chilling reminder for some; for others, that looming finish line is seen from a different perspective—a beautiful reminder that because life is fleeting, it is therefore invaluable and precious.

As children, we knew what it meant to be alive and enjoy the moment. We knew how to laugh, play, and lose ourselves in the little breaths of life that being alive offered. We felt that energy constantly, finding entertainment in even the most mundane things, and would pursue the things that interested us. This is how we learned what we were passionate about. Looking back on these childhoods now, we laugh, because all those little moments have turned out to be our most precious memories. Moments like jumping off of cliffs and playing soccer with kids. Unfortunately, so many of us are so busy growing up that we forget to hold onto important childhood qualities. There's a point in the road where we're so focused on where we're supposed to be heading that we forget what's right in front of us and how to enjoy it. We often lose our true selves through the winding roads of change and wonder just what happened along our journey that made us so stale, bitter, and generally not all that fun. We tend to grow bitter at the world rather than see opportunity in it.

To grow up isn't a bad thing; we just have to make sure to not lose sight of our best youthful qualities. As children, we were who we were, and we completely owned it. We could find incredible amounts of fun every day, even when adults could see nothing but a bore! We were happy with talking to the new kids at school openly and we forged new, sometimes meaningful, friendships more easily. This opened our path to new opportunities and experiences that we would have never experienced before. Is it any wonder we made more friends in our childhoods? Is it any wonder why life seemed longer? If we made mistakes as children, we learned from them and weren't embarrassed by them until we were taught to be. Most of all, we had a passion for living and a curiosity for learning that left us when we became adults.

With increasing age also comes increasing responsibility, which for a positive-minded person also means more, not less, opportunity to pursue interests. The best part of growing from youth into adulthood is that opportunities to pursue our passions are not only much more available to us, but we are in more control of which of those dreams we want to chase. As adults, it's much easier to travel to the places we've always wanted to see and to try the things that we've romanticized since childhood. We open ourselves up to new ideas and create new habits, and with this openness to the world comes an openness in our minds to learn, accept, and expand our horizons.

Growing up doesn't extract fullness from our lives; it's growing up while forgetting where we come from, what it was like to be a kid, that does it. If we take the time to let our inner child come into our lives, we can find that carefree, life-filled perspective again. We don't have to grow stale, boring, and grumpy just because our years are moving along. We can choose to grow more fun, happy, and energetic instead!

To open your eyes wider on your journey, to see opportunities you've never been able to see, to climb new mountains previously laden with mist, and to bathe in rivers previously deemed too wild to swim in is to unleash your childlike spirit of play. If happiness is your kindling, play is your tinder. You can never build a proper fire without both of these things.

A commitment to play, helps cultivate the spirit of discovery. When we are immersed in what lights us up, we are in a better position to open our eyes to the richness of existence and the possibility that surrounds us. It is significantly more difficult to find our way in life if we aren't in a positive mental state. Unleashing your spirit of play and embracing pura vida should not come after we know what we want to do with our lives—it should come before. Besides keeping your eyes open to the possibility of future ventures that you may be passionate about, play is essential to adding zest to life, boosting creativity, relieving stress, promoting learning, and most importantly, connecting you to other people around the world who are like you. After practicing happiness, you must commit to pursuing what makes you come alive, whatever that is. If you don't know exactly what it is that makes you come alive, be physically engaged in discovering it. Make a bold decision to lean into it. Don't just wonder if you think rock climbing, writing a book, or entrepreneurship is for you—embrace pura vida and do it! If you stop at wondering, you'll be wandering your whole life.

When you concurrently practice happiness and play, you will be in a blissful and inspired place, and that place will guide you much more clearly to discovering what it is that you want to do with the rest of your life. So, what one massive action can you take today to begin existing in that inspired place? There is only so much that these words can give you. They can create the curiosity that will help you find your purpose, but you have to make the journey.

The beginning of an extraordinary life starts with nobody else—it begins with YOU! Nobody else will do it for you. Nobody in this world will push you very hard to live a life that you love; you must do it yourself and for yourself. Make a promise to yourself that you will finally quit thinking about taking action and actually do it. If I've learned anything while traveling, it was that the best way to get anything done is to just go ahead and do the thing—to quit talking about going to Chile, and instead just book a ticket, get a visa, pack your bag, and let the magic unfold itself. After you take one action, settle into it, enjoy it. What opportunities are there now? Are you noticing different paths that pique your curiosity? Take another step and make it a little more focused this time. Be a little bolder in the subsequent steps; get out of your comfort zone, if you're interested in it. I mean, the comfort zone is fine, but you will never grow just sitting there, dwelling in it. I promise you this: if there is anything more powerful that I have learned in my life, it is that you will never learn your limits until you have the courage to test them. Your old patterns must be challenged in a big way for lasting change to happen.

If you want big change in your life, it's a good idea to make a big change within yourself and jump off the cliff into the ocean of life. You must quit saying that you will "try" and start exclaiming loudly and boldly that you "will."

Pura vida . . .

CHAPTER FIVE:

A Grand Perspective

"The sacred lies in the ordinary."
—Deng Ming-Dao

I. Celestial Curtains

One of my most profound moments while traveling, and one that I love sharing with fellow travelers who ask, was also a moment that redefined my perspective on life and the abundant beauty in the world—a moment that shifted my sense of adventure and opened up the possibilities of living deeply and presently.

When I was about eight years old, my brother and I would spend many evenings playing video games. As adventure for most eight-year-olds is often confined to the vicinity of the home, we would imagine ourselves going on the great adventures that we found in our video games. One particular evening, we were completely transfixed and lost in a world where we were guiding Mickey Mouse through all parts of the world to rescue his dog, Pluto. After a handful of hours, we had gone far enough in the game that we made it to the "ice level" (as

many video games of the era were known to have). While playing the game, I became less focused on what my character was
doing in the game and more fixated on what was happening in
the environment onscreen. I recall that the background in this
level had what looked to me like glowing green curtains floating largely above the horizon, covering the entire night skyline.
I asked my brother about it, and he explained that that was the
northern lights, a real phenomenon that existed in some far-off
corner of the world. I was in shock that something like this
actually existed in real life. There couldn't be any possible way
that something this beautiful and impressive actually occurred
outside of an imaginative video game. I sat and pondered that
only great adventurers and explorers would ever be so lucky to
see something so beautiful in the real world.

As the years went on, I played fewer and fewer video
games, and developed more and more interest in the wonders
of the world. I became even more enamored with the northern
lights—the aurora borealis. I would spend countless hours gazing at pictures in books and learning about the science, causes,
and legendary folklore of the lights. I grew increasingly inspired
and anxious to see them myself someday. One of the Norse
myths I read about said that the northern lights were believed
to be reflections from armor and spears of warriors coming to
battle. As a kid, this kind of legend only filled me with more
romance and adventure. Over the years, I learned more about
the actual science behind the aurora borealis—solar winds
interacting with the Earth's magnetosphere—but rather than
demystify nature's greatest show, this knowledge only interested
me more. As I grew older, I decided that I needed to stop just
dreaming about seeing them, so when I created my bucket list
in my early twenties, without any hesitation I wrote, "Finally
see the northern lights," in the number-one spot.

As I went through my twenties, I was fortunate enough to cross a lot of items off my list, but "finally see the northern lights" always remained unchecked. Ultimately, I kept talking myself out of it every time I reviewed my list, because the lights are known to be elusive and it can't be guaranteed you will see them even if you do make the trip. The Auroras always seem come with a lot of luck for most of those that do see them, and it would take a large investment on my part just to try even once. It wasn't until I was coming on my thirtieth birthday that I decided I could keep dreaming about it or finally just go for it. In a quick moment—much like the one in which I had booked my trip to Japan—I booked a flight to Iceland to cross off the number one item on my bucket list.

I arrived in Reykjavík, Iceland, a name that roughly translates to "Bay of Smoke" or "Smoke Cove," on a frigid December day (or at least the clock said it was day). As I landed, I noticed that the entire sky was painted a pitch-black, as it would remain for twenty hours a day at that time of year. From what I could see through the darkness, the beautiful, untouched, and sharp landscape was completely covered in ice and snow. From the airport window, Iceland was exactly how I had always imagined it. Once I exited the airport and stepped foot in this new country, I felt the cold biting in a way I had never experienced before. This was a long way from my sunny Southern California home—or any place I'd ever traveled to before for that matter. One thing you notice as soon as you take a stroll in this city, besides the incredible natural beauty, is the people's love of art and their heritage and history. I decided as I arrived in my hotel room that I would do nothing in Iceland until I found the northern lights. I was on a mission, and I planned on being persistent. After a quick power nap to try to take care of a small amount of jet lag, I headed out into the dark, howling winds of the land of fire and ice to a bitterly cold, barren, and snowy beach.

It was the middle of the night in a country far from home, and there I was, standing on a desolate beach, with my eyes planted to the sky, searching for the northern lights. I waited, gazing skyward for close to three hours, but there was absolutely nothing. The waves were crashing on the beach, the winds were howling, and while I was wearing no fewer than three layers of jackets and thick thermal shirts, I felt practically frozen. Cold, wet, and jet-lagged, I was about ready to give up for the night, trying to convince myself in some strange way that it "just wouldn't be right" if I had seen them my first night. *Maybe the challenge will make it all sweeter when I finally do see them*, I reasoned.

As I was thinking, suddenly a bright green light streaked across the pitch-black sky directly over my head. At first, I thought I was seeing things—after all, it was bitterly cold and I was still partially jet-lagged—but then, in the span of about thirty seconds, the entire sky began to light up in a vivid and luminous neon green that started dancing like a Norse god's curtains over the ocean. Breathtaking, vivid, surreal, and illuminating are the best words I could use to describe this experience, but words ultimately cannot convey what I saw or felt. This show lasted for a full hour. The auroras were beautifully framed by a massive lighthouse on my left and an almost full moon out into the sea, like something out of a painting. No—better than any painting. These brilliantly illuminated celestial curtains were breathtakingly vast but seemed to dance and flow weightlessly through the night, painting a clear and starry sky with vivid green auroras and neon sparks of velvet purple crackling off its edges. The glow wrapped my view from all sides, high enough to reach the moon, but close enough to almost reach out and touch, it seemed. Green and purple sparks flowed like a river in the wind, flickering softly through the darkness, kissing the ocean and swimming in the heavens. This night was alive with a fire in the sky that shined with awe-inspiring color. It was the most breathtaking thing I have ever seen. When it all started, I couldn't speak—nor did I even try. I just stood there, dumbfounded, feeling as if I were in some sort of numb dream. I thought I'd seen the beauty of the lights in books and videos, but nothing came close to actually experiencing them. I could not believe how gorgeous they were, and how alive they made me feel. I had seen hundreds of videos and pictures, but to actually be there in the Arctic snow—freezing cold, on my personal quest in an opposite corner of the world—was nothing short of life changing. Even the locals described the lights that night as epic. I took no pictures—I wanted to just be there, completely alive and in the moment, appreciating nature's incredible beauty right in front of me. I knew the memory would provide itself.

After an hour of seeing the greatest show on earth, the lights began to fade as quickly as they had appeared, and ultimately they disappeared into the night sky, leaving nothing but a memory for me to witness on a snowy, desolate beach. On the way back to my hotel, I reflected on the whole experience. It already felt like some sort of vague dream that was difficult to fully grasp. As a child, I had mused that I would have to become a great explorer or adventurer to ever be lucky enough to see one of the seven natural wonders of the world—especially something as breathtaking as the aurora borealis—but here I was, just over twenty years later, finally fulfilling that dream. I smiled, thinking that my eight-year-old self would have been proud of the adventure I had lived and the man that I had become. On the bus back to the hotel, I wrote a small poem in my journal:

Swim among celestial curtains,
Hidden beyond the edge of the world.
The Earth has wisdom for those who seek it.
From wonder to wander, it speaks to the soul.

I closed my journal, smiled, and decided to head into town to celebrate with a beer . . .

My bartender's name was Aurora.

II. The Greatest Show on Earth

Reykjavík was a welcoming city—as it of course would be, being one of the safest cities in the world. Traveling to a country I had never been to before, to a place where I knew absolutely no one, the warm people I met were a welcome relief from the biting cold and the freezing winter air. Wandering the streets reminded me of trying to navigate the streets of Tokyo, of matching Kanji symbols on train signs with the map I was holding. With the streets in Reykjavík named things like Hverfisgata and Klapparstígur, trying to remember the directions people were giving me or following my own map became a monumental task, since I didn't speak any Icelandic.

Sitting at a coffee shop almost every morning and going out for a dinner every night, I got to know a handful of the locals very quickly. Initially, with most conversations I had with locals who I thought may be open to discussing it, I tried to satiate my desire to finally know once and for all if Scandinavians actually believed in trolls and fairies, but of course, I never got a straight answer, or at least nobody denied they existed. After discussing Icelandic folklore, I discovered that Iceland has a bit of a thing for music, as almost everyone I met was a musician and played in a band. As a musician who was open to the possibility of talking about trolls over a black coffee, I naturally bonded with just about everyone I met. But one particular guy I met at the Lebowski Bar—yes, named after the film—in downtown Reykjavík stood out among everyone else.

Alexander, like almost everyone else in Iceland, was a musician, and like even more people in Iceland, vague on an answer if trolls and fairies were real. I was beginning to enjoy the mystery of it all by this point. Over a couple of pints of my new favorite Icelandic brew, Einstök White Ale, we talked about much more than trolls or music. As we sat cozy in the pub, locked warmly away from the big snowstorm outside, the night rolled on effortlessly. "Gluggaveður," I learned, is the word Icelanders use to describe this type of cold weather—stunningly beautiful, but best enjoyed through a window, in the warm confines of a home or pub.

I shared my story of experiencing my lifelong dream of seeing the northern lights just the night previous. I shared every detail, every tingle in my body, and smiled and laughed through most of the story. Here I was, getting chills just telling the story about that night, never mind actually experiencing it again. I was speaking a mile a minute, as if I were a kid excitedly opening gifts on Christmas morning.

"You know, hearing you tell this story, I see how excited you are by it." Alexander paused and smiled. "We see the lights so often around here, sometimes I think we forget to remember just how beautiful they really are."

Of course, this shocked me. Here I was experiencing something I viewed as nothing short of a gift to humankind—the greatest show on earth and a phenomenon I had dreamed about since childhood—and here was this guy saying that people of Iceland often forgot how beautiful the lights truly are.

"How in the world . . . ?" I asked (not even a real question). "If I had something as stunning as the auroras in my own backyard on a consistent basis, I would slow down and be in complete awe of it every single time."

"Well," he replied, "maybe you have something back home that we would feel about in the way that you feel about the lights . . . and maybe you take it for granted sometimes?"

A definite and defensive "no" was coming out of my mouth, but before I actually said anything at all, I thought of my home. And in thinking of home, I thought of the very thing I often take for granted: the Pacific Ocean that sits right outside my front yard every single day. I pretty much grew up in saltwater, spending my whole life no more than a thirty-minute drive from any beach at any given time, and while I still enjoyed and loved the water, maybe I *was* taking it all for granted? I considered this thought.

Alexander was right; just as the northern lights appeared often enough in northern Scandinavia to become "normal" to most Icelanders, another one of the most beautiful sights in the world, the Pacific Ocean, had become "normal" to me. This was a profound sadness, and as strange as hearing that a local Icelander felt that the northern lights had become "normal."

I laughed at the absurdity of missing out on such an incredible beauty that's around me all the time. There's beauty that is all around us; it surrounds us every single day. It's just that we become too acquainted and comfortable with it to appreciate its full grandeur. Through constant alienation, we become bored with the world, and eventually the world in our eyes is robbed of its color. I realized that the northern lights were, of course, a stunning display of the beauty of nature, but that the true beauty of nature puts on a wonderful show all around us, all the time—it's just up to us to slow down and see it for the beauty that it is. There's equal elegance in the ocean as there is in the northern lights—as there is in a mountain, as there is in a flower. All of these are the universe manifesting itself in some way. It's just easy for us to lose touch with how beautiful it all is. There's magic everywhere, at all times. We can dramatically expand our lives not necessarily by adding onto the number of our years, but rather by deepening the fullness of our moments, by simply recognizing the beauty and sacredness that is all around us. It's up to us to take notice, no matter how insignificant we think it is.

We wrapped up our drinks at the Lebowski Bar and walked the cold and dark streets of Reykjavík for hours, sharing stories about our lives and inspiring each other to step more boldly into our futures. We found seats on a bench by a park and played music together, writing a song late into the night—Alex on the guitar and me on the Irish tin whistle.

III. The Truth About Trolls

Sitting in a coffee shop on my last day in Reykjavík, I found myself next to a large, muscular, long-bearded man. He reminded me a bit of what I imagined the Norwegian explorers looked like as they first settled here—a Viking if I ever saw one in person. This, I admit, excited me greatly.

I greeted him.

"Hello!" he replied, stern faced but obviously open to some conversation.

"Tell me," I asked, not reluctantly at all, "I've been obsessing over this for years. Do you believe in trolls and fairies?" I laid it out there.

"I do not believe," he answered, with no hesitation in his thick Icelandic accent. Finally, one way or another, I had an answer!

But he continued, ". . . because I know."

Okay, now we're cooking here, I thought.

A long pause.

I sip my coffee; he sips his beer.

"So, what happens when you see fairies?" I asked, hiding my excitement.

"You can only see them in nature . . . camping, in the wilderness."

This guy seemed to be pretty level-headed and intelligent, and I sensed no sarcasm in his voice. I was going to cross off the number-two item on my bucket list and finally learn the truth about trolls and fairies in Scandinavia! I couldn't believe my luck!

"And what do you do when you see trolls and fairies?" I asked.

"Fairies? Let them be." The modern-day Viking sipped his schooner of beer and set it down on the bar. "When you see a troll," he continued as he slowly turned his head to me, "you run the other fucking way!"

And that was it! I finally had my answer and we toasted to trolls, fairies, and the northern lights!

"Skál!"

PART II:

THE EXPLORATION

CHAPTER SIX:

Knowing Where You've Been

"Nothing ever goes away until it teaches us what we need to know."
—*Pema Chodron*

I. Golden Buddha

Life can be complex, I know, but by taking the time to understand the story of our lives, we help bring beautiful new insights, clarity, and ideas about the person we authentically are, and begin to create leverage into understanding exactly what it is that we were destined to do. The person we identify ourselves as today is usually a culmination of our experiences, our roles in life, our loves and our interests, but too often, as life begins to get more hectic and demanding, we tend to overlook and even forget important patterns and circumstances that have influenced and shaped our lives.

In our society, we are so focused on just getting by that we too often tend to forget the really important and impactful elements of our lives, those little memories or interests that hold an immense amount of potential for discovery. Frankly, life gets hectic, and we slowly forget who we are. life becomes routine, especially in the outcome-focused, go-go-go mindset of our world. Because of this, it's very likely that you don't remember or have overlooked important parts of your story that have influenced you as a person, because immediately after the event happened, instead of relishing in and reflecting on the beauty and perhaps even meaning of the experience, you urgently went back to focusing on something else.

Unfortunately, small or large, the experiences you've likely forgotten are affecting you today, oftentimes without your awareness. By simply becoming cognizant of your life story, from the beginning to the present, you can uncover some important insights regarding where you would like to take your life. By looking at your life from an outside vantage point and laying it all out on a measurable timeline, you can see your story from a more detached place, and thus, see more objectively and with less ego involved. When viewing the story of your life this way, it's likely that you'll become aware of a subtle string of events, a certain pattern that led you along in life and began to shape the person you are today.

By taking some time to get to know and understand your past, you will see where your life may be trying to take you in the future—almost as if you had finally awakened to the path that the entire universe was begging to show you, a path that's been right in front of you your whole life. When we take the time to revisit our life stories, we are able to take notice of the plots and possibly uncover where they're leading.

I get emails all the time, from all over the world, asking me for advice on how to discover purpose. In these emails, I'm usually expected to give some sort of clue that's out there in the world to be found, and as a result these people are understandably confused about why they're unable to discover a life of purpose.

"I thought I found it, but I'm bored of this path already."

"I just want something that lights me up."

We all seem to be looking outside of ourselves for purpose, but purpose is not found outside of ourselves—it never was! Purpose is inside us, and it's been there our whole lives—we've just forgotten how to listen to it calling us. The beauty of purpose is that it works from the inside out, not the outside in. It's like spending your whole life searching for your glasses and realizing they were on top of your head the entire time. We think purpose will call us from out there in the world, saving us from ourselves, but it doesn't work that way. Even when you travel the world looking for some sort of meaning in life—like I had done—that isn't how we actually find purpose. It's simply that wandering far enough from the world we're accustomed to and into strange and curious places that allows us to gain clarity and detachment from what isn't us and thus, allows us to get curious with ourselves. Often something from the outside can spark that "aha" moment, but those moments are only ever a spark of what was already within us our entire lives. It's not about adjusting to the outside world; it's never been about that. It's about connecting to what's on the inside and boldly stepping into that. We just have to open our hearts and embrace the adventure.

But discovering where the universe is asking you to go is not about adding more to your life; it's about taking away what's burdened you. There's a story that I love telling people, about uncovering your authentic self in your past. It is the story of the golden Buddha. Way back in 1957, a group of monks in Thailand had to relocate their monastery to make room for a new highway in Bangkok. During the relocation, the monks began moving a ten-and-a-half-foot, two-and-a-half-ton clay Buddha. One of the monks noticed a large crack in the clay of the Buddha, and when he looked closer, he saw there was a bright golden light coming from the crack. The monk went back into the monastery to get a hammer and a chisel to chip away at the clay. Slowly, it was revealed that the giant Buddha statue wasn't made of clay at all; it was made of solid gold. Historians believe that hundreds of years earlier, as the Burmese army was attacking Thailand (called Siam at the time), Siamese monks covered the giant Buddha with clay to keep it from being looted by the Burmese. While the monks were viciously slaughtered, the ten-and-a-half-foot-tall Buddha remained, because the Burmese thought it held no value. It wasn't until 1957 that the golden Buddha hidden beneath all those layers of clay was finally discovered.

You are a lot like this golden Buddha. Within every single one of us lies our very own gold, trying to shine through all that crap that's been layered onto us throughout our lives. All we have to do is chip away at that clay, piece by piece, and realize our powerful inner potential. And you know what? That golden Buddha has always been there, and uncovering it is much easier than any of us realize. Throughout our lives, however, incredible amounts of proverbial clay are layered over our inner golden Buddha. Limiting beliefs are adopted without test or logic; societal expectations are followed without much question; cultural pressures are accepted because we want to fit in; and other external influences—even our own unconscious conditioning—begin to define us before we understand who we are. By the time we're old enough to start thinking for ourselves, we are so loaded down with clay that we forget who we really are—we lose our golden Buddha. But when we finally free ourselves from society's expectations of who we should be, we liberate ourselves to become who we are meant to be.

An important key to finding the golden Buddha that lies within us, to finding the purpose of our future, lies in our past. All we need to do is begin chipping away at that surface-level clay, like the Siamese monks in 1957, so we can make room for our authentic inner selves to shine.

II. Lessons from the Australian Outback

In my first trip to Australia, I had an experience of further uncovering my own inner golden Buddha. Since I was a child, I had always been fascinated with the "land down under." I watched *Crocodile Dundee* religiously—as if that was any indication of what authentic Aussie life was like—and I begged and pleaded for a pet kangaroo one Christmas. I learned how to play the didgeridoo, the ancient aboriginal wind instrument, and even learned how to toss around a boomerang. (I guess it's no wonder that the woman I'm dating, Jessica, is an Aussie.) Yeah, I loved everything about Australia, so I figured it was high time to make my trek down there.

Once I landed, Jessica and I began a five-hour road trip deep into the outback wilderness. As we drove through the desert, I had my face planted on the window, just like I had done on my first trip to Nicaragua. Seeing all the kangaroos hopping around the red landscape was magical to me, something—like the northern lights and the Norwegian fjords—that I had always wanted to see and was finally getting the chance to. This is one small reason I love travel so much: it allows us to see the world in a new light, like we're seeing the world for the first time again.

We eventually found our way to a little outback town called Hawker (but don't say it like "Hawk-ER," say it like "Hawk-Ah"; otherwise, as I learned, you sound like a tourist), located in the Flinders Ranges of South Australia, with a population of a little over two hundred. We stopped in a local pub, had a drink with the bartender and chatted about the farming life in the town, as Australia's favorite country artist, Slim Dusty, played over the jukebox, singing about the woes of a pub with no beer. After a quick pint, we drove off into the red outback dust, into miles of dirt roads, venturing even deeper into the desert to camp for the night.

Together, Jessica and I set up our camp as the sun fell below the vast horizon, embracing the largest mountain range in South Australia. We lit our fire to keep us warm in the freezing desert winter. I'm willing to admit that she proved to be a better fire starter than me, which was a pretty big deal for me, as we were a new couple. While my ego may have been bruised, I was impressed. As we lay on top of outback soil by the crackling fire, sprawled out warmly under a thick Mexican blanket, I looked up at the sky. Foreign and mysterious constellations I had never witnessed were draped over us—southern stars. I had camped my whole life but had never had the gift of seeing the night sky so clearly in the Southern Hemisphere. Not only was the Australian land alien to me, but so was the sky. Orion was replaced by the Southern Cross. I had never slept in nature with such a clear view of the sky before. I was in utter astonishment—under foreign skies, I felt farther away from home than ever, but also closer to myself.

The next morning, we awoke to a friendly wallaby hopping around just outside our tent, and a thin layer of ice covering our blankets. Beautiful. After a cup of much-needed hot coffee made over a morning fire, we drove farther on into the outback of the Flinders Ranges, to a place called Sacred Canyon. The walk into the canyon was along a dry riverbed that lead to a spring. This spring was where the aboriginal people, the Adnyamathanha, gathered around to tell their stories and engrave their art into the rocks. It's believed that the engravings at Sacred Canyon are thirty to forty thousand years old, and their art is still in that canyon today.

I learned that for the Australian aboriginals, walkabouts are a rite of passage where males of a particular tribe venture into the outback on foot to live on their own for as long as six months. This is done to attain a spiritual enlightenment and to transition into manhood. Now, can you imagine, in this age, turning off all your electronics, leaving everyone and everything you know behind, and trekking into the wilderness to live there for six months? What do you think would happen to you? How would you respond? Walkabouts are a concept that's incredibly foreign to us, with our gadgets attached to us at every moment, constantly waiting for that next email or that next social media notification. I know this difficulty from experience. As a result, we have not only become disconnected from nature, but we have also become disconnected from ourselves. What usually happens to the aboriginal men during their walkabout is that they become more connected, not only to Mother Earth, but to themselves. They learn who they authentically are because they let go of distractions from their lives for a significant period of time, in order to listen to what their souls are trying to tell them.

Walking through Sacred Canyon and seeing the ancient aboriginal cave paintings, thousands of years old, reminded me of how important it is to turn off distractions and expectations, and to turn inward—to listen carefully to the own sound of our hearts and to what our very being is begging to tell us. We simply can't do that when we are constantly checking our phones and living by someone else's standards, thereby allowing that proverbial clay to keep stacking up. It's simply impossible.

Of course, you don't need to go on a walkabout through the Australian outback to discover your inner golden Buddha—all you really need to do is put away your distractions for a period of time. During my first Australian adventure—before I moved there—I made a pact to keep my phone off for the two weeks I was there. No phone calls at all, and I decided to check email only once per week. If you wanted to get ahold of me, you probably had to wait until I came back to the United States. I wanted to rid myself of distractions in order to further find myself, to chip away any more clay that I was carrying around with me. By this time, I was already life coaching and living my purpose, but I was living my purpose in a very vague and inauthentic way. It wasn't until I allowed myself to be with me and to listen to my heart without expectation or social influence that I discovered what kind of life coaching I was meant for, who I really wanted to work with, and how I wanted to show up in the world.

Prior to this trip, my coaching business was pretty successful. But I was coaching from a model that wasn't entirely me. Even though I had found my passion, I was doing it in a way that I believed would make others happy—in a way that I thought would make me successful. This was a typical case of cultural influences governing my decisions, even if it was on a more subtle level. The thing was that I wasn't thrilled with the type of coaching I was doing. It was incongruent with who I really was. During my trip to Australia, I had the time to self-reflect—because I rid myself of distractions—and during that reflection, I realized that while coaching was in fact my calling, I needed to coach more from a place that was me and less from a place in which I hoped others would accept me for.

The interesting thing about this situation is that I immediately started to coach and present myself in a way that was authentic to who I was, whether or not I thought I would be successful. I quit sharing stories of successful executives and started sharing stories of adventurous people who inspired me. I quit speaking from a pre-made framework and began speaking from my heart, no holding back, no matter how offbeat people thought I might be. The great paradox in this is that when I quit doing what I thought would make me successful and started following my inner golden Buddha, I became successful. Go figure.

III. The Story of a Lifetime

Consider for a moment the entirety of your own life—all the beautiful memories, the lessons learned, the life-altering moments, the high school loves, summer memories, years spent meeting new people and learning new things. Slow down, take a few deep breaths, and just take it all in. Let the flashbacks of your life come flooding into your mind without any judgment. Sit with your story for as long as you like. Watch it as if you were watching a film of someone else's life. What is the story being told? Is it epic? Is it funny? Is it exciting? Is it emotional? How do you feel about your life's story? When you're finished, slowly open your eyes, and beginning at your birth, make a list of and evaluate all the significant events that have occurred in your story all the way to the present. Spend as much time as you'd like writing them out.

When you are finished writing the basic blueprint of your life's story, it's time to summarize your list. It's important to encapsulate and simplify events that are similar so that we can more easily notice patterns that have presented themselves and to search for some meaning or what you've learned within those experiences. For example, if you moved a lot when you were a child, sum up that experience by writing, "Moved a lot during my youth, and I learned to be resilient and versatile as a result." During your school years, you might write something like I did when doing this exercise: "Attended high school and discovered I loathed economics and math, but discovered that I really loved English." Simply seeing how much I loved English influenced me to begin writing more. That single, subtle insight hidden away in my life is what led me to write this book, in fact. Oftentimes you will find greater meaning than you may think in the subtle details. It's important to acknowledge the big events in every part of your life. I've found the best way to do this is to divide your life by key moments. For example, birth to grade school, then grade school to twelve years old, then your teenage years up until you are twenty-one years old, and then every decade since. This method helps you narrow down and focus on every part of your life story, whether you feel like there is something important there or not. Add as much as you can remember and take your time reflecting.

Once you're finished, take a moment to review your life story on paper. This is my favorite part, as there's so much nostalgia running through my mind, remembering events that might be decades old. Go through the list you have made and star key events, the important lessons you've experienced—both negative and positive, major and small. Notice the turning points, and important people who have helped shape who you are today.

Moving forward, it will be important to stimulate your mind and to help you open your eyes to certain threads and patterns that have run throughout your life. Some of your answers may lead to possible careers, interests to pursue, or qualities to help you grow. Answer these questions with an open heart, authentically and unabashedly expressing your best self. Take pen to paper and write out as much as you can. Take your time in an inspiring mental place and let the barriers come loose, just for a moment. Sit at a place you enjoy; pour a glass of wine or a cup of coffee; play some music that lifts you up and puts a smile on your face. A few words or sentences is just fine, but oftentimes the real diamonds are found in the detail, so be as thorough as you can. If you realize you're repeating answers in different questions, that's a good thing! That's exactly the kind of thing you're looking for!

What do you see as big turning points throughout your life? Being aware of how your life was shaped, either through external forces or by your own doing, can help you gain great clarity as to the person you authentically are, your own golden Buddha. What kinds of patterns do you notice in these turning points?

What lessons were you taught throughout your life? Too often, there are profound lessons that presented themselves in the past and that we have so far failed to understand or notice. It's easy for us to overcome a difficult challenge and just be happy that it's over and done with; however, these challenges and difficulties often have invaluable treasure within them, if we only take the time to reflect on them and open our eyes to the wisdom this moment was trying to give us. What would happen in your life if you began to view every challenge as a call to a great adventure? When you reflect on your past challenges, whether or not you immediately see an opportunity for learning, ask yourself, "If this moment were disguised as a lesson just begging to teach me something, what would it be asking to show me?" Put a positive-minded spin on not only your happiest, but also your darkest moments, and you will be surprised at the incredible light you will be able to uncover. Remember, it's not about throwing away your proverbial teapot. It's about allowing the scars to be illuminated, learning something from them to become better and even more beautiful as a result of having been broken in the first place.

Reviewing your list, do you remember what you wanted to be when you were younger? Perhaps there's something valuable in recognizing what that dream career of your youth was. It's possible that that career is still something that would really light you up, and it's actually likely that there is an element of that potential career that you would still enjoy. What specific aspect or aspects of this youthful dream attracted you to this kind of job? When I was younger, I wanted to be a detective, an astronaut, and even the president of the United States. Upon reflection as an adult, I realized that actually being any of those things wasn't what was important to me, but it was what each of those things offered that called to me. I didn't really want to be the president of the United States, I just wanted to lead and inspire people. In wanting to be an astronaut, I spent time uncovering why I wanted to do that when I was younger, and I discovered that it was more about satiating my spirit of adventure and exploration—two ideals that have greatly influenced my coaching. See, it wasn't being the president or an astronaut that I wanted, so much as a life of leadership, hope, exploration, and adventure. Why did you want to become what you wanted to be when you were younger? Are there other careers out there that you could pursue that could offer you the same type of satisfaction? Knowing what you know now, which careers, or even parts of them, are still calling to your heart?

What really pumped you up, lit your soul on fire, and energized you in your life? Maybe, like me, you found being outdoors in nature to be completely exhilarating, or maybe you loved to bury yourself in books at the library, learning all you could in a single afternoon. Again, my love for the outdoors not only influenced my style of coaching, but so did my constant lust for knowledge. Is there something to be uncovered in your past that you've long since abandoned and that really made you feel fired up? If it energized you, then there's a good possibility that it may offer the same charge now. Part of discovering your life purpose is to quit settling for what you have to deal with and to start being engaged in what truly energizes you. It's much easier to get out of bed every morning doing something that fills your batteries up rather than drains them.

Viewing the story of your life, if there was something you had given up on, what would it be? Be completely vulnerable and honest here. This kind of pondering may be humbling and emotionally unpleasant, but what lies on the other side has the potential to hold something very enlightening. If you died today, what would you regret not having done?

Now that we've spent some time getting more clarity on your story and delving into the history of your life, let's take a look at who you are today—and most importantly, who you want to become. It's going to be important moving forward to be really honest with yourself and listen to your heart, to sound out the distractions and expectations surrounding you and to practice what I call "no-limit thinking." This phrase means to really dream big, as if there were no restrictions on your life—no fear, no chance for failure, and all the money in the world.

Accordingly, it's important to think in a way that cultivates an imaginative mind, so you can get rid of the ideas that prevent most people from dreaming big (let alone living big!). What one great, epic, and amazing dream would you dare to live if you knew you 100 percent could not fail, and if there were no obstacles on your path to greatness? What would you do with the rest of your life if you weren't scared? This concept of failure prevents so many from seeking out greatness that most never take the first step on their journeys. Assuming that failure was impossible, what is it that you would do? If your happiness paid the bills, what would you do with the rest of your life? Let's take not only failure but also money out of the equation. Seeking a life of only financial riches is what gets most people into emotional trouble in the first place, so just imagine that the amount of joy and happiness you experienced on a daily basis directly influenced the amount of money in your bank account. What would your life look like? What would you be doing on a daily basis?

What is it that truly and deeply inspires you in your life right now? What makes you feel as though life is a great, fun, and beautiful adventure? What part of life makes you feel most energized and impassioned? What do you currently enjoy about your work? No matter how seemingly depressing and miserable, there is always something about anything to be happy about, no matter how small it may be. Think hard here; I know it's there. In your heart of hearts, what do you really want from your career moving forward?

What hobbies or interests do you have right now and what hobbies or interests did you have during childhood? What are your absolute favorite things to do? What really makes you lose track of time? What kinds of activities would you take up if you only had more time, more money, and more freedom to actually do these things? I'll tell you right now, I used to want to climb mountains, go cliff diving, and surf more, if I only had a little more time and money to do these things. When I committed to actually doing these things, however, I found there was always enough time; I just had to make the time. And there was always money; I just had to realize the importance of doing these things and then sacrifice what wasn't filling me up to make room in the bank account for what could! What is it specifically that lights you up about these hobbies and interests?

Who is your ultimate role model in life—living or dead, a person you would most want to be like? What kind of amazing magic do they have that you don't quite possess yet? Where is the gap between who they are and who you are, and how can you begin to close that gap?

Now, let's take it a few years into the future—well, a lot of years, probably. Imagine you're at your ninety-fifth birthday party and your family is all surrounding you, telling stories about all the amazing things you've accomplished during your life. As you're blowing out the candles on your birthday cake, what do you want these stories that your grandchildren are telling to be about? How do you truly want your family to remember you? What do you want to be remembered for? Do you want to be a person who laughed things off, even during the hardest times, or do you want to be remembered for your sour attitude? Maybe you want to have lived a life of complete service, or perhaps you think hearing your family talk about how you spent so many years teaching yoga and healthy eating in Bali would be a life worth writing about!

Let's take the concept of being remembered a (big) step further from our family—to the entire world! Consider what your legacy would be if you had no limits. How would you want the world to remember you? What do you truly want the rest of your life to be about? If you had a message to share with the world, what would it be? What would you be willing to die for? What do you think your big dream is? How do you think you could earn money while living this dream?

What have you just realized about yourself that you may have forgotten or never even thought of? What have you learned about yourself overall? You should now be able to notice a theme uncovering itself. What are the commonalities, building blocks, or key pieces of information you noticed from your answers? Be sure to listen to your heart for the answer, not your ego. If you're feeling overwhelmed, this is a good thing—you've just uncovered something very powerful and potentially life-changing about yourself. Now it's up to you to take some sort of action, to create this life. It's likely that your mind has a list of possibilities to pursue, and that, again, is a good thing. You don't have to jump full-on naked into the river of life quite yet. Sometimes just getting your feet wet is a good start.

Finally, taking in your entire life story—all your memories, lessons learned, and experiences, good or bad—what does it look like you've been in training for? What do you see that your life has been heavily focused on? What does it seem like your existence has prepared you to do with the rest of your life? This answer may come as an "aha" moment, or it may take some deeper reflection to uncover. The answer, like searching for an ancient lost city in the Amazon jungle, is oftentimes not too obvious at first glance, but with persistence and patience, it will be unearthed. Take some time away, quiet your mind, and your heart will begin to speak.

What really stands out to you now that you've revisited your life's story? What have you learned about who you were, about who you are, about who you will be? The way forward is often accelerated by seeing what has propelled us in our lives. You have been the main character of your own story your entire life; now it's time to write something worth telling.

CHAPTER SEVEN:

Finding "the Way"

"Be yourself—not your idea of what you think somebody else's idea of yourself should be."
—Robert Edwin Lee and Jerome Lawrence

I. Breathe, Breathe in the Air

Life for me used to be a constant battle with my mind, always going at one hundred miles per minute. I used to always think about what could happen wrong in the future and, if I wasn't thinking about that, I was thinking about all the ways I've messed up in my past. As a result, I was always on edge, restless and distressed. The beauty of life was aflame all around me, and I was focused on everywhere but life; I was focused on everywhere but the present. After all, the very foundation of depression is when we perpetually live in the past, and the foundation for anxiety comes from always living in the future. What was the answer here? Well, on a cold winter night on the beach in front of my home in Southern California, I learned that the answer was to simply be present.

Shortly after my trip to Iceland, I found myself in a bit of a self-inflicted ordeal. I was finishing the lease at the place I was living and did not really know what I wanted to do or where I wanted to go next. As a result, I got rid of most of my stuff—save a few dozen of my favorite books, a couple of surfboards, and however many clothes I could fit in one armful. I threw what I had left in my small Toyota Scion, and decided to settle into a position of sleeping in my car for a few weeks to get my head straight and figure out what I wanted to do. My mind and heart were calling me to two different places. I was at a turning point in my life; I just didn't know which way to turn.

I had called it off with one woman I was dating at the time, and while I wasn't particularly heartbroken this time, this breakup was a strong wake-up call for me. She lived in New York, so we would occasionally fly the three thousand miles to come see each other, but the distance ultimately proved to be too much for both of us. On our last visit together, she flew out to California. We went out for a day trip to Santa Monica and we both knew it was over. It was a final goodbye of sorts. One of the last things she said to me was, "Travis, you're too smart to go through life just settling all the time." Those words alone were something I held on to for a long time. By the time she left, all my friends were moving on to their own careers and were either engaged or married; even my fellow lost boy, Marcus, had just tied the knot himself—in a wedding where I got to cross off another bucket-list item, since I officiated it. We all had little, if any, time to spend together anymore and I felt pretty alone. This time, though, I felt more alone than I'd ever had.

It wasn't like the first time, however. I had a sense that things would eventually work out—I just had to figure out how, and which direction I wanted to travel in. A part of me wanted to go to . . . I don't know where, somewhere else to live—anywhere else. *Maybe Alaska, maybe even Spain*, I thought. I spent a lot of that year reading Hemingway, so his novel *The Sun Also Rises* gave me some inspiration to travel to Spain. Another part of me, however, was second-guessing myself, wondering if that was just me trying to run away from my problems and loneliness.

Sleeping in my car offered me a uniquely offbeat sense of freedom. Part of it was a fun little novelty, almost playing the part of a modern Jack Kerouac character. The other part of it was wildly lonely. Late on my fifth night of having my car as my home, I couldn't get myself to sleep. I realize that a driver's seat isn't the most comfortable place to try to get some rest, but I'm famous among my friends for my ability to knock out just about anywhere. After a couple of hours of tossing and turning, I resolved to just head to the beach to look up at the stars for a while. I drove by the nearest all-night diner to get myself a hot, black cup of coffee and made my way to the ocean.

As I sat on the sand and sipped on my coffee, I began to notice how scattered my brain was. I became aware of my thoughts as my mind grew more and more anxious, thinking about what the hell I was going to do with the rest of my life—*where am I going to live, what's in this coffee, what's the meaning of life, when is the car registration due again—seriously, this coffee tastes like cardboard, what's in it—what happens when we die?* I grew more despondent as my mind wandered into thinking about all the lost years of my life that I wasted on trivial pursuits, and wondering how things would've turned out had I done that one thing just a little differently, or how I was settling into a life when I was "too smart for that." My mind was everywhere it could possibly be except for the one place that mattered or that spiritualists say is real . . . now. Right here, right now.

Everyone at that time assumed that I meditated because I spent so much time in nature—or maybe because I often wore mala beads around my neck and wrists—but I had, in fact, never meditated at all. Sitting alone on the beach in the middle of the night, I considered that this might be the perfect time to start. I didn't know much, but I had heard an Alan Watts lecture on it once, so I thought I would give it a shot.

Sitting upright on the sand, I crossed my legs, laid my hands on my knees, and closed my eyes. "Watch the breath," I remembered Alan Watts saying. *Watch the breath*, I silently said to myself.

Watch the breath . . .

Watch the breath . . .

As the gentle sound of the lonely night waves lapped up on the sand, I gradually and deliberately began to let my thoughts go. As they entered my mind, I purposefully returned my awareness to my focus, my breath. When my mind wandered, I acknowledged it and returned to the breath. After a few minutes, I became interested in the different sensations that breathing created in my nose, diaphragm, and chest. Such a small breath, such a large life force. After a few minutes more, I became interested in identifying the exact moment my in-breath ended and the out-breath began. I wasn't trying to not think—I knew that was impossible—but I was working to become conscious and aware of my thinking, and as a result, I slowly began to see myself not as my thoughts, but as something more. After about twenty minutes, I felt briefly what it was like to not have labels, even the self-associated ones. I wasn't my thoughts, I wasn't any of that. Briefly, I just . . . was.

What am I going to do with the rest of my life?

Back to the breath.

Why did we break up?

Back to the breath.

You're never going to amount to anything, Travis.
Back to the breath.
What the hell was in that coffee?
Back to the breath.
Breathe . . .
Breathe . . .
I bet the ocean looks beautiful right now.
Back to the breath.
Breathe . . .
Breathe . . .
Breathe . . .

I sat on that cold January sand, on my very first meditation, for forty-five minutes. Then I opened my eyes and did something completely unexpected. I began to laugh like I hadn't laughed since I was a small child, like a real honest-to-goodness pura-vida kind of laugh. You know those deep belly laughs that hurt because you can't stop, and then the absurdity of all the laughing makes you laugh even more? That's the kind of laugh I had on this beach. I was sure that if anyone had seen me, they would think I was a crazy bum going even crazier, but I didn't care what anyone would think of me. I wasn't defined by what others thought of me. Hell, I wasn't even defined by my own thoughts. I wasn't anxious—at least I didn't feel anxious. I didn't feel depressed, either; these were merely things that I chose to keep carrying with me throughout my life. Through my contemplative stillness, I was separated from the everyday clamor and finally allowed to hear the subtle sound of my own heart. So much clarity and insight came from that one meditation, from just sitting and being. To let go of distraction for a small amount of time allowed me to see into my very being, to see more clearly who I was—not what the world was expecting me to be or to do. And because of that night on the beach, I've been meditating almost every day since, connecting more and more with every meditation into my core, my values.

II. The Discovery of Self

At the end of the day, the most important part on our journey of self-discovery is to first understand what it is that we stand for, what we believe in, what makes us . . . well . . . us! The best way to get clarity on what makes us "us" is to find something that we truly believe in, to get crystal clear on what we value.

If you've been beaten down and gone through life trying to please everyone but yourself—working to play it safe and secure and keeping that "settle" mentality—then there's a very good chance that what you value will be much different from the road you're currently on. If you're living out of alignment with your values, you're living someone else's life, and if you're doing that, then you are not living your own. It's rare that anyone knows their own set of core values, but perhaps you already know yours, and if you do, you want to make absolutely certain that these values are in fact your own and have not been simply conditioning throughout your life.

Over recent years, it has become increasingly difficult to be fully with our own minds. Never mind trying to weed out others' opinions of what we should and shouldn't be, but technological distractions have approached enormous levels as well. It has become much easier today to be anywhere other than where we are in the moment, mentally speaking. We are more connected on a technological level than we ever have been in history, but because of this, we are more emotionally disconnected with ourselves than ever before. As a consequence, we perpetually struggle to find meaning in our lives. We can't fully be with what our hearts are trying to tell us, because in the backs of our minds, we are waiting for a beep from our phones, constantly immersed in the petty distractions that surround us. We are actively sacrificing rich lives in the name of interferences that essentially zombify us. We are becoming less mindful and more mindless. We must make it a practice and a habit to liberate ourselves from these technological distractions, and we must become strong enough to take control of our minds, so that we may listen more closely to what our hearts are calling us to do.

The idea here is to think without the expectations that anyone else has given to you. Even thinking this way can sometimes be difficult, as we're constantly surrounded by distractions, extrinsic pressures, and ideas that are not our own. I thought I had my values dialed in for a couple of years, but it wasn't until I started spending more time with my own thoughts in Australia that I was able to clearly see what it was that I valued. I started hiking on my own and meditating more frequently, partly so I could better see who I was authentically. It is important that your thoughts and ideas are your own, and also to be sure that when you approach these practices, you make time for you.

If you read about or talk with any extraordinary people who have ever lived, you will find that there are common themes and values that recur across most of their lives. Some of these values are a blend of wisdom, courage, love, spirituality, and many more along these lines. If you haven't yet gotten clarity on what's important to you, take your time—close this book, find some quiet in an inspiring place. Turn off your distractions and spend a moment reflecting on and thinking about it.

In Western society, we are conditioned from an early age to place most of our value in money. We pursue it relentlessly and at all costs, even sacrificing our happiness and health to get it. We are constantly seeking to accumulate more wealth in a never-ending quest to get that raise, so we can buy an even bigger yacht than the one we already have. We are wildly proficient at placing this religious importance on money. We know "money can't buy happiness"—at least we tell ourselves that—yet we're surprised to look at our seven-figure bank statements and see that the bonus check didn't come with happiness. Money may not be the root of all evil but seeking a life of nothing more than monetary wealth is the root of stagnation and ultimately emotional demise. When we sacrifice our spirits for a paycheck, we cannot ever expect anything more out of life.

Are you living in a way that positions money as your top priority? This is a normal attitude, but how does life look ten years from now if you continue to live with money as your top value? Making money is great—don't get this idea twisted—but is what it takes to make the money enriching and rewarding to you, or are you settling into something and biding your time until you can retire, working at a place you hate as a means to an end? Are you enjoying the part of your life that you spend making money, or is it something you feel like you have to do so you can make enough income to pay the bills and have a little left over to let loose a bit on the weekends? If you're placing money as your top value, you are in for a rude awakening, as money has no intrinsic value. Of course money is a part of my own life and it's nice to have money, but it can never come before your core values—otherwise you ensure a life of boredom, pain, and regret.

For example, as you may have guessed, adventure is one of my core values, so if I had enough money to buy a house in every country and a swimming pool to go with each house and then still enough for my great-grandchildren to live lavishly, but didn't have adventure in my life, I would rather die. And I would rather die in this case because I understand that what lights my heart up has more value to me than money does.

What lights you up in your life has more value than money, whether you know what that value is yet or not. If I couldn't live in alignment with adventure and my other core values, I might as well be dead, because that's exactly how I would feel.

The big question here is whether you are working closely with what you care deeply about or whether you are sacrificing that for a paycheck. Even if that paycheck comes with seven digits and a massive Christmas bonus attached to it, is it really worth it? Are you creating something truly meaningful to you and the world, or are you just passing away your time here until things can maybe become a little easier for you one day? Are you on a journey through life, doing something great that will not only lift you up but also put a dent in the world, or are you surrendering your core values to support the values of some giant company with values that aren't even your own? Always remember that if you don't stand for something, you will fall for anything.

Within every single one of us lies a boundless space of wisdom, and this inherent wisdom is best accessed through silence and by quieting your distractions so that you may openly listen. You know more than you think you do; it's just a matter of learning how to listen to your heart and rethinking the way you see yourself. You have an inherent wisdom—now you must spark and unleash it. A simple seed grows into a mighty tree by growth from within. Just like this small seed, your very calling is within you, to be grown into a mighty tree from that seed that you already hold. It should be watered and nourished from the surrounding ecology daily, but not born that way.

Our thinking becomes best expressed when we are centered and present in the moment. The most straightforward way to connect with our hearts and let our inner wisdom guide us is through silence. I personally use meditation—as it has had a dramatically positive impact on my life, well-being, spirit, business, and relationships—but you can use any form of silence. I cultivated this type of uninterrupted silence by taking walks to nowhere in particular, surfing by myself at predawn hours, and going on long hikes. You can call it sitting, mindfulness, meditation, or prayer—whatever works best for you. The intention of this type of mental stillness is to give you a moment to silence yourself, to turn off the distractions, regroup, and listen. When you quiet your distractions, your heart will begin to whisper. When you quiet your mind, your heart will begin to sing.

Start by quietly observing your thoughts, emotions, and feelings. Suspend your judgment, put your preconceived ideas and beliefs on hold, and just watch your thoughts. This already is an incredible breakthrough, as we are so used to being surrounded by everyone else's interpretations of what the world is and what you should be. Simply quiet your mind and listen for who you are, if you can. Do not listen for typical survival pleasures like sex, money, and power; listen for something higher, for who you really are. Consider that we are happiest and living most with purpose when we are living in a way that is natural to us—that is to say, living in alignment with our authentic selves. To live authentically by who you are, not what culture expects of you, also means that absolutely no effort is required. Listen to your heart but be quiet for a while first. Ask questions, then feel the answers. Learn to trust what your heart is saying; it is your heart, after all. Self-discovery necessitates soul-searching and reflection. Nobody is going to define your calling for you; this is your journey.

Once you have a basic understanding—no matter how vague it may be—of what makes you come alive, let's get a little clearer in a very practical way. Spend some time—I usually say between ten and fifteen minutes—writing whatever inspiring words you can think of. These don't have to be any type of words in particular—whatever you can think of that lifts your spirit up—write it down. The words can be people, places, actions, things; they can be phrases or hobbies, or they can be books or movies you love. As long as they make you feel connected to them in some way, these words can be anything you desire. Take some time getting into an inspired and positive mental state, and just let your heart and soul bleed onto the paper. Allow your inhibitions to go and let it flow. The major goal of this practice is to bring up that childlike mentality and just let the words come out of you—no judgments and no barriers, only freedom and genuine expression. Simply letting your mind wander and allowing your heart to express itself without borders can often-times reveal ideas about you that you've been long-conditioned to forget.

Now, look at what you've written down on your paper. Which of these words hit you as the most meaningful to your heart? Circle fifteen words that most make you feel something inspiring, that resonate with you or maybe put a smile on your face. Say these words out loud to yourself—how does it feel? Saying these words should make you feel better than saying the other words you have listed. As of now, we will consider these fifteen words some of your values. You don't have to stay with these values forever, but this is what you'll move forward with for now.

The big goal here is to be you, 100 percent, authentically you! When defining your values, don't force yourself to be like someone else, even if they are somebody who you look up to. Don't try to fit your values into a pre-made mold of what the world expects, and don't judge yourself based on what makes you unique and rare to this world. The world has enough people following the same stagnant path that everyone else seems to be following. What the world desperately needs is an adventurer of spirit. The world needs who you authentically are, and it needs you to unleash that! Defining your core values will not only help you come alive, but it helps the world come a little more alive as well. If you need a little extra inspiration here, consider who you really admire and identify what you think their values are. Do any of their values light you up? Add them to you list.

We're not quite done yet, though—we haven't yet discovered your *core* values, the things that make you come most alive! So, I want you to laser this list down even further. Now that you have your fifteen values, we have a much better concept of what it is that you identify with and stand for. But just because you stand for these values doesn't mean they are your core values. Therefore, we must find the five values that most resonate with you. Take some more time in that inspiring mental place to uncover which of those fifteen values can become your absolute core values, the ones that are most important to you, the ones that would uplift and inspire you if you were to live a life that embodied them. Is this an easy exercise? Not always—in fact, most often it's not—but the more you can see what's important to you, the more purposefully you can live. Core values are like a fingerprint—they're different for everyone, so it's important to pay close attention to what *you* value, what makes you authentically *you*, not what you think other people value or what you would be accepted for! There's only one you, after all, so why not completely own it and be the best version of you that you can be instead of wasting life trying to be someone you're not?

III. Living with Harmony and Integrity

Understanding what you value is a massive step toward not only walking down a life path that lights your heart on fire, but walking down one with a bit more intention, to open your eyes to one that may fulfill you. Once we know what we value, we need to actually live in alignment with that. How can you figure out what it takes to create a life where you're working toward living in complete alignment with your values?

In my years of meditation and reading about Eastern philosophies, I've discovered that, in the Taoist philosophy, the universe is considered like a river. In Tao, you are not swimming in this river, but you are the river itself. The Tao understanding is to freely flow in the direction that the river is taking you and not to exert yourself by going against it. Going against the flow of life will cause you absolute discord. What would seem to be the paradox here is that when you relinquish control, you gain all control. You must be like the river in living in the flow of your values, keeping your eyes open, and allowing your values to take you where they may flow. If you are constantly fighting against the current, you'll bring about absolute discord and disharmony in your life and, as a result, even the world. Your purpose is like your very breath; you do not have to tell your body to breathe—it just does, much as the ocean does not have to tell a wave to crest and break. Your destiny and calling are the same way. Your heart is calling you in a direction like the river that flows; it's up to you to listen to your inner self, to listen to your heart and follow where it is taking you.

Discovering your core values is one thing; living in alignment with your core values, however, is the more challenging part. The big distinction of success in any area of life is not in the knowing; it's in the doing. Just because we're clear on who we are doesn't mean that we are any good at acting in harmony with that. As a famous Christian saying goes, "There's a fine line between Saturday night and Sunday morning." How many people do you know who say one thing and do something entirely contrary to what they say? Besides being hypocritical, this is called "absolute discord," living a life out of alignment—a life where you are anxious, depressed, and have a deep, unsatiated longing for fulfillment.

"Absolute harmony" is the opposite of absolute discord. To live with absolute harmony is to live in a way that consciously aligns your being completely with your core values. A life of harmony is a life of happiness, bliss, presence, and total fulfillment. There are three distinct practices to living in alignment with your values and gaining absolute harmony in your own life—when what you do, what you say, and what you think are fully congruent with one another. Your beliefs, your words, and your actions should be harmonious and consistent with one another, and when your actions are in alignment, you have learned a beautiful practice: how to live in harmony with your essence. This practice can oftentimes be very challenging to the newly initiated, but it is the same concept as adding weight to your bench press or adding five minutes to your meditation practice—the more you test yourself, the easier it is, and ultimately, it becomes who you are without you trying anymore.

Now it comes to the truly life-changing work, a matter of learning to live in alignment with these things. Easier said than done, sure, but like anything worthwhile, a challenge is the best place to grow. The day I committed to living in alignment with my values, my life grew in a purposeful and abundant way. The world became much more beautiful, and life much richer. The space between absolute discord, where you possibly are now, and absolute harmony, the place you want to be, is called the "integrity gap." The formula looks like this:

Absolute Discord ----- Integrity Gap ----- Absolute Harmony

Absolute harmony is your highest inner potential; it is where purpose becomes much clearer and fulfillment becomes a daily part of life. It represents your unlimited self—someone who lives with honor, respect, and complete integrity. Absolute harmony, when achieved, is the pinnacle of who you are, living in complete alignment with your core values and thus independent of society and cultural expectations. People who have absolute harmony are boldly and easily expressing their authentic selves to the world. When living in complete alignment with what you believe in, you're living life to your fullest authentic potential. You're living life your own way, flowing through the river of life with ease and grace—not in the way that society, your family, or culture expects you to, but in a way that you expect yourself to. After all, Mahatma Gandhi himself said that "happiness is when what you think, what you say, and what you do are in harmony."

It's possible that you believe one thing about yourself, but you speak in a way that is contradictory to that belief. Maybe you tell your friends that you are a mellow and peaceful person, but the truth is, you're getting into arguments anytime you all go out together. There is no clarity among what you believe, what you say, and what you do. Your consistency of integrity can manifest itself in many different ways. You can say that health is important to you, but spend every other lunch driving through a fast-food chain.

The bigger those inconsistencies are among your values, the more miserable you are inevitably going to feel about life. Your first step in becoming consistently congruent with your values is to slowly and surely close that space between what you value and how you live. You will notice that the smaller your integrity gap is, the more easily harmony will express itself in your life and the better you will generally feel. And when you are living in complete alignment with your values, consistent in what you say, think, and do, you will be living in absolute harmony. This path is not necessarily linear in the beginning. We must remain vigilant so as not to backtrack into absolute discord again. Remember that weeds don't need much water to grow, but beautiful plants certainly do. Over time, if you practice and remain cognizant of progressing along the path, living in alignment with your values won't be something you have to be vigilant about so much as something that will become second nature.

Reflect for a bit here and think about the moments in your life when you are most aligned with your own values. If one of your core values is fun, think of when and where you're having the most fun. Wherever that is right now, you want to work on spending as much time there as possible, so you close the integrity gap and live more in alignment with your heartbeat, your purpose. It is important that you are engaging yourself in what supports your values on a consistent basis. Now, reflect on when in your life you are least aligned with your values. Spending too much time here, as most of our society easily does, leads to absolute discord; we are out of alignment with our values and oftentimes in complete contradiction with them. So, if one of your core values is fun, uncover when you are having the least amount of fun. It's important to recognize when you are not living in alignment with your values so you can consciously take steps away from those activities and people. Do these two exercises with the rest of your core values and see what you come up with.

What are you not doing in life that, if you started doing it, you could be more aligned with your values? What small steps can you take today into that life? You don't have to make the big leap right away, but after getting clear on what your values are, it's important to begin thinking, speaking, and acting in alignment with them. Are you living somewhat congruently with your core values, or are you completely inconsistent? Decide one small action or habit that you can make to begin your journey toward absolute harmony. After that action becomes a habit, take another step, and another after that.

Begin to design your ideal life around your core values and not your circumstances. Pay close attention to when your heart is really singing—when you feel most alive, when you feel most happy and most purposeful—and take another, more driven step in that direction. Continue doing this until you are fully embodying your core values.

There will be times when life will throw a massive storm at you. There will be challenges, and like the mythical hero's journey, there will be beasts to overcome. There will be moments when you can't quite see your destination and aren't even sure if you're lost. But knowing your core values and choosing to live congruently with them is like having a compass on your journey that will always point you to your true north. Even if you become lost on your path, following your inner compass—your core values—will eventually lead you to your purpose, like the river of life leading you to the El Dorado of your soul.

CHAPTER EIGHT:

Ikigai

"Don't ask yourself what the world needs; ask yourself what makes you come alive. And then go and do that. Because what the world needs is people who have come alive."
—*Howard Thurman*

We must not ask ourselves what the world needs—that kind of questioning only leads to settling into something that may not be what lights us up—but rather, we should ask ourselves the more profound question: "What makes me really come alive?" I mean, really dig deep and consider what it is that makes your heart sing. Asking first what the world needs is like asking yourself, "How can I make money?" You become very limited in your thinking, your options seem scarce, and unconscious barriers begin to present themselves, potentially closing you off from your purpose and what will light you up inside. As to finding our life purpose, when we ask ourselves, "What can I do to make a living?" our answers become reactive instead of reflective. Our answers will usually come down to describing the job we are at right now or, my personal least favorite, the uninspired answer, "I don't know." It's important to get rid of the dead-end questions we're accustomed to asking and begin asking more powerful questions that can create leverage—questions like, "What truly makes me come alive?"—and choosing to simply do your best to do that very thing. Like Howard Thurman said, "What the world needs is people who have come alive."

Embarking on your adventure of purpose and finding your true north is what the world so fiercely needs. We have enough bland, meaningless careers out there; what is desperately needed in this world is for you to stand in your power and bring that passion to the world. There are people out in the world who—whether they know it consciously or not—need exactly what your inner compass is pointing you toward. Who are you to take that away from them? I believe it is our duty as human beings to spend our time here making an impact in the world, and that can only be done by doing what lights us up.

Growing up, I had many passions—traveling, exploring, surfing, hiking the wilderness, studying astronomy, playing soccer—but I limited myself by always asking the default question, "What can I make money doing?" Inevitably, my answers were either what the people around me were doing for a living or something that I cringed at the prospect of doing for the rest of my life. I grew up this way, thinking this was just how life was supposed to be. It wasn't until my midtwenties, when I chose to do some inward reflection and self-discovery, that I began traveling the world to find some answers. Through my world travels, I also stumbled onto another philosophy that had an even greater impact on my life. Outside of finding some answers on the question of happiness, I also discovered a bit about purpose.

Before leaving on my trip to Japan, I chose to read and learn as much as I could get my hands on about the culture there (save for learning the language). One late night, I stumbled upon *ikigai*. The philosophy struck me, as it is defined as, "a reason for being." As I explored further, I discovered that the Japanese believe that everyone in the world has their very own ikigai, but discovering my own would require some deep soul-searching. Ikigai is a quadrant of questions designed to elicit thought, pondering, and ultimately discovery. This was a concept I chose to allow myself the time to explore more personally on my trip to Japan, and I knew just the place to do it.

Shortly after my day getting lost in the streets of Kyoto, I took another train about an hour outside of downtown Tokyo to climb a peak in the city of Hachiōji—Mount Takao. The mountain was a relatively short climb, standing at 1,965 feet tall. I spent the early morning slowly trekking up this mountain and beholding the stillness of stunning wilderness surrounding me. There's a lot of folklore associated with Mount Takao, and while it sadly had nothing to do with trolls and fairies, it was associated with spirits of the surrounding mountains and forests, particularly kami, which are spirits worshipped in the Shinto religion. From my understanding, kami are typically described as elements of the landscape that are not separate from nature but are of nature. Walking up Mount Takao, I thought about the surrounding folklore and the "spirit of nature," which gave the climb, on this cold March morning, a certain mystical and otherworldly quality, especially as the fog began to creep slowly up the ridge and seep through the trees and onto my path.

My main mission on this hike—outside of my wanting to be fully present in nature—was to work on discovering my reason for being, my own ikigai, upon reaching the summit that morning. As I summited, I looked down through the fog at the city of Hachiōji, basking in the cool but welcoming air. I was surrounded by cherry blossoms and a perfectly wide-open view of Mount Fuji appearing through scarce clouds in the distance. *A classic place for some soul-searching*, I thought as I pulled out my worn and trusty red journal from my back-pack, drawing the ikigai quadrants . . .

My (and your) ikigai is right there in the middle of all those interconnecting circles. The idea is that if you are coming up short even in one area, you are unable to discover life's true purpose. The most important questions in finding your true north are simple, yet they take time and deep self-discovery to uncover. You must be engaged fully in that which you love, in that which the world needs, in that which you are good at, and finally, in that which you can be paid for.

Ikigai is that intense internal burning to pursue your personal mission; finding it, according to the Japanese, is not only the key to discovering your purpose, but also to a much happier and longer life as well. The Ohsaki Study, a prospective cohort study done in 1994 had tens of thousands of Japanese adults surveyed, showing that almost 60 percent of the participants had an ikigai. Besides having a purpose and feeling happier, they reported lower levels of stress and better health. Having a reason for being—the place where passion, mission, vocation, and profession meet—means that life has a beautiful meaning. This philosophy is also why so many Japanese never really retire (and why I don't ever plan on retiring myself)—because they are too busy doing what they honestly love.

Your passions are more than random things that happen to interest you. The things you get excited about, that you love, or that make you happy are not some passing fancies you should just ignore or only pursue when you have free time. The things you love and the things you are good at are signs of what you are perhaps meant to do with your life. You must first contemplate what your true passion is and maintain the attitude that you can do what you love with your life. The question does not ask what you can make money doing—that is a weak question that will only lead to weak answers—it simply asks, what are you passionate about? Pay close attention to what lights you up; make a list of these things and decide which of these you are most passionate about. When you look at all of your passions, at first it might seem like there is no association among them. Odds are, however, that you can merge what you are passionate about into a single idea. When you are clear on what your passion is, it will become easy to work for, because you enjoy it and it won't feel like work.

Next you must ask what the world needs. If you are passionate about something, there is a guarantee that others are passionate about it as well. Let your unadulterated authenticity shine through, because there are people out there who want exactly what you have to offer. Consider what people, businesses, or communities could want or need that you are passionate about. Perhaps they already know they need it, or maybe they don't know yet. If the world doesn't know it needs what you are passionate about, this is an opportunity for you to be a pioneer. There is a gap in the market for what you will create; you just have to define what that gap is and who needs it. Create an attitude of service, so that you may give what you love to others.

What are you good at? What are the strengths you already possess? Are you not especially good at what you're deeply passionate about? That's all right, too—everything, and I mean everything, is learnable. You can learn to be good at anything you set your mind and heart to. If you don't feel like you're good enough at your passion to make a living doing it, ask yourself what are the skills that would make you exceptional at your passion, and how you will go about learning them. Practice this passion often—learn and read books about it, surround yourself with like-minded people. You will read books that will teach you something new, or meet people who may provide opportunities or give you a step up.

This is all great and fine—I'm sure it's very inspiring for you right now—but how can you actually be paid for all of this? Notice I didn't ask, "Can you be paid for this?" as that question only contributes to mental barriers. I want to know how you can be paid for it. Your passion is not an antithesis to making money, like some of the world would have you believe, but it is a beautiful opportunity to make money. If you've found the gap in the market by uncovering how the world needs what you have to offer, then coming up with a way to become the gap in the market should be quite simple. The best way to answer this question is to ask how you can give what you love to others.

These questions aren't necessarily meant to be asked one after another, but rather to be reflected and meditated on as a whole. When I sat on the top of Mount Takao in the mist, surrounded by forest, I conceptualized practically dozens of different answers for each of the four questions—and that spirit is exactly the main idea here. The answers won't come easily or automatically, nor should they. I sat on top of this mountain for a long time, pondering dozens of different answers for each of the questions before I had my own eureka moment. After the morning sun had passed beyond the trees, I saw that my underlying passions in life were adventure and inspiring others; I was exceptionally good at listening and pushing others to better themselves—oftentimes annoyingly so—and I saw a way I could make a dent in the world, by helping people come alive and live a life on fire, because I felt that's exactly what the world so desperately needed. The funny thing is, my ikigai was really right in front of me my entire life. Having powerful life-changing conversations was something I was so passionate about and, frankly, really good at. Whether I realized it at the time or not, years of bartending taught me a lot about actively listening and lifting up people who needed it. I loved having those kinds of conversations; I relished them every time I had the chance. I could have these types of inspiring talks about possibility for the rest of my life, without a break, and still be happy. What held me back was that it wasn't so obvious to me how I could make money doing this. At the time, I didn't know what life coaching was, but I was determined to follow the path that had seemed to open up for me, the path my heart was leading me toward, and I trusted that the money would eventually follow. My heart had yet to fail me. I would go forth in the world from Mount Takao, figuring out how to have powerful conversations for a living. Do not rush this, as it should be something reflected on over time. Dig deep within yourself, let your barriers fall, and think like a child. Upon discovery, you will have your own eureka moment.

I. That Which You Love

"What is the meaning of life?"

Of course, there is not one single answer to this question. The meaning and purpose of life can and should be different for everyone. The better question perhaps is, "What is *my* meaning for life?" What I have seen with myself and with those whom I work is that the purpose of life seems to be going boldly into the world and doing what makes you come alive, because that tends to be exactly what the world needs anyway, or at least what *someone* in the world needs. The way I see it, even if you only change one person's life, you have changed the world on some level—you have made an impact. What's really the point of living if we're not enjoying this gift of life in some form or another? We are best able to give to the world, to make a meaningful dent, when we are engaged in what makes us come truly alive! Ikigai is all about joining our interests and passions with what the world needs, so again, before we touch on what the world needs, let's explore what makes us feel most alive.

There are things we absolutely love engaging ourselves in! We are naturally drawn to certain activities, hobbies, or even ways of thinking. These are the kinds of activities we completely lose ourselves in. When you hear people talking about "flow state" or "getting in the flow," they are usually engaging themselves in these kinds of things. In the adventure of purpose, one of the most important places to look into is your own passions! Purpose involves pursuing something of meaning, yet that meaning should also be in conjunction with what we feel like we were destined to do. As Buddha once said, "The master of the art of living makes little distinction between his work and his play."

Too many well-intentioned people only reserve their hobbies and interests for that much-anticipated weekend, or even worse, they never engage in their interests and passions at all. More still have no idea what their interests even are! We convince ourselves that we're far too busy with life's "important" to-do lists, our chores, and our work hours to have much time for anything else, let alone active engagement in what we love. But you will never, ever discover your life's purpose—what makes you really come alive—by just thinking about what you love. You will never find your calling by dreaming about it, and you will never be able to listen to what your heart is trying to tell you by just reading this book, putting it back on the bookshelf, and letting it collect dust. If you're considering just thinking about or even reading your way toward your life's purpose, forget it—it won't happen. You must actually act upon it and start living it. Be fully engaged—physically, mentally, and emotionally—in discovering it for yourself. And that's the really fun part. That's where life becomes interesting.

You can be delivered the keys to the castle, be given all the wisdom this world has to offer, but it is entirely up to you to embark on the quest to find that castle. If you are lost in the woods and there are five trails, but you have no idea where any of those trails lead—let alone which one leads to your final destination—what will happen if you decide not to take any trail at all? What will happen if you choose to stay put right where you are? Staying where you are only leads to stagnation. Nothing extraordinary will ever happen. Nobody will ever come to save you from yourself, and for the rest of your life you will remain wondering what could have been. You can never find your castle and you will never discover your purpose. In this spirit, you must choose to take the trail called passion, and take it as soon as you see the opening. Will this trail lead you toward your calling? Maybe, maybe not, but the point here is that you are actively and purposefully moving—you are taking action! If this particular trail leads you to your calling, fantastic; and if it doesn't, there will be many other forks in the road that you wouldn't have found if you never moved at all. You can always choose to turn back to take a fork in the trail, or even still, you may decide to blaze your own trail entirely. But it is impossible to discover yourself and your calling without having the courage to first embark on the journey. You may not know your calling yet; in fact, odds are you don't, but actively pursuing your passions and interests will greatly guide you in self-discovery.

So, what, in fact, are your passions? If you don't feel that you have passions in life, that's not true—you just haven't awoken them yet. What are you interested in? If you don't know, what would you like to try for the first time? What did you love when you were younger that you've given up on? What truly moves you? Taking money out of the equation, what could make you get up in the morning excited to start your day without hitting the snooze button over and over?

Maybe your passion is writing, or maybe you're interested in skydiving, but lately you haven't read any more books on the subject and you certainly haven't strapped on a parachute and jumped out of a plane. Maybe you've always wanted to try traveling, but there's not a single stamp in your passport. Or maybe you always thought it would be interesting to hike the Appalachian Trail, but you've never had the courage to take the three months off of work to do so.

I'm not asking you to strap on a parachute, find yourself the nearest cliff, and start BASE jumping this week; and I'm not imploring you to quit your job today so you can finally walk the Appalachian Trail, but if that's what interests you, I would have you consider the importance of taking the small steps in that direction. I am telling you that you must be engaged in what you love, or could love, even in a small way, so that you may see your purpose more clearly. Passion isn't just an attitude; it's a way of being actively engaged in what you love with the spirit of being fully present in it and simply enjoying it. You must take the first steps onto the trail that most piques your interest. Join a group, read about these interests, take surf lessons, take a poetry class, commit to a weekend getaway camping with your friends, get a gym membership, take a course in tantra, join your local soccer league—do whatever it takes, just be sure to move! Be engaged in what sparks you so that, eventually, the fire will light within you and your wild thing will run free.

Remember that watching movies, sleeping in, and Sunday-funday mimosas with your friends are probably not the answers we are looking for here. All of these things are fine, but without some actual meaning in your life, these things—yes, even Sunday-funday with your friends—can become boring and unfulfilling in the long run. These things are the ways in which you spend your time, not the ways in which you engage in your purpose. So, explore the possibility of activities that could give value to the world and others, so that you truly come alive! So, what do you love? What are you passionate about? What makes your heart sing and your soul come alive?

What makes you come alive? What fulfills your soul?   I mean really fulfills you and lights your life on fire? What would you wholeheartedly love to do on a regular basis that will employ your skills and interests, and which of all these things could really add substantial value to the world and to other people's lives?

If you're not quite sure what you're passionate about or even interested in, a great way to find your passion is to get rid of the money mindset; after all, the simple goal of making money is what gets people into a soulless mess in the first place. If you inherited one hundred million dollars overnight, what would you do with all of your time, after you've traveled the world and crossed off all your bucket-list items? If you had all the resources, all the time and money in the world, and everything at your disposal, what would you engage yourself in?

II. That Which the World Needs

Ikigai is the most powerful reflection you can do on your adventure of purpose, and perhaps by now, you have a dozen new ideas about where you can go, or maybe you're still unsure. The preeminent question that will help you clarify your direction is, "What does the world need?" Or even, "What can I teach?"

Asking the question of "what can I teach?" is an effective exercise because it helps expose areas that you're good at, or that you could be good at it. Believe it or not, you already have value to give to the world—whether or not it's obvious to you yet, it is there. If you're vague on what your value could be, a bit more self-discovery is important. I had my ikigai pretty dialed in when I went to Japan, but going even deeper a year later helped me get even more clear on the types of challenges I can help the world tackle. You will find that you have a lot more to offer than you thought. You're already a pretty amazing person—and no, I'm not putting you on.

So, what is it that you can teach? What do you know right now that others will want to learn? Don't just stop at what you can teach right now, though—that is often another limited way of thinking. What would you like to teach if only you knew how, or were a little better at it?

Take a moment to consider something that is not usually so obvious to most people: What do others already ask you to help them with? Maybe what you're good at giving is not necessarily something that you even notice right now. Consider some of the challenges you have overcome in your life story and the lessons that you have been taught throughout your life. Which of these challenges will others want to learn about overcoming themselves and what kind of challenges can you help people overcome?

I love working with people who want to make a dent in the world and a positive impact on the way the world lives. Whether that's on a scale of changing the way entire nations do business or even on a singular level—changing one person's life—it's all changing the world in some way. What do you believe the world so desperately needs right now?

III. That Which You Can Be Paid for

It's easy to feel awkward when it comes to commingling our money with our passions. Over the course of our lives, we become conditioned to think that selling ourselves out is the only decent way to make money. After learning this type of lesson, it's easy to believe that if we're engaged in our passions, then we shouldn't try to make any money doing it. I dealt with guilt and self-sabotage myself, when working to mix my passion of helping people with making money. Who the hell was I to want to make money while trying to change the world? But making money is an essential part of surviving. Everything in this world has a value attached to it, so why shouldn't you give value to what you have to offer?

If you are ever going to make an income doing what you are passionate about, it is necessary to provide enough value that it solves others' needs. Money has everything to do with how much of a dent you make in the world—that is to say, how many people you impact in the world. Solely doing what you are passionate about is not enough. If we're unable to add value to other people's lives, we can never create a life doing it.

Think about your passions for a moment. Really press yourself—do some research if you have to—and consider: What are five audiences out there in the world that would love to learn your passion? Is your passion something you can teach to a group? I worked once with a man who was deliriously joyful about painting. He lived and breathed art, and was constantly talking about it with the kind of fervor you have when you talk about a new lover. Even our sessions together were always about art. He was looking to change careers and do something more meaningful with his life, something that really fired him up and would maybe fire others up as well. He was always told that painting would never pay the bills. He was in a position where he loved painting but would never want to make that his actual career, as he saw it as therapeutic and relaxing and didn't want to mix any kind of money with it. On finding his purpose, I simply asked him, "Who can you teach your passion to?" That question helped open his mind to all sorts of possibilities. He now teaches painting in workshops.

Why stop at what you can teach, though? What could someone be willing to pay you two hundred dollars an hour to do? Maybe your own art could be worth good money, if you only learn to market yourself right. It could be that teaching something isn't a concept that fills you up inside. If you could do what you're passionate about while getting paid for it, what would that look like? What kinds of skills would you need to improve on? Is there a potential business that could be built around what you love?

What do you have right now that others could be willing to pay you for? Again, don't be limited in your thinking. Ask yourself an even more powerful question: What could you have right now that others would be willing to pay you for, if you only put the time and effort into learning it or making it a reality?

IV. That Which You Are Good At

Every one of us on this planet has an incredible magnitude of talents and skills. However, it doesn't always mean that we are supposed to use them all in discovering our purpose. Just because we're good at something does not mean that it will bring us fulfillment. It could be that you're gifted at cooking or talented with public relations, but does that mean that these are your purpose? If the skill doesn't bring you joy, then the answer is no. If it does bring happiness into your life, consider it further. There might be certain things you're good at and that you enjoy doing, but that aren't part of your life purpose. These could be things that you just enjoy doing on weekends, and that's perfectly okay, too.

Reflect on and dig deep into your own talents and skills, and consider what comes especially naturally to you. What are your major strengths in life? What are you already good at? If you're unclear on exactly what you're gifted in, start getting social—quit being so modest and ask some of the people around you, your family and friends. You may not be able to see what you're a complete rock star at, but a fresh clarity can come from the outside looking in. These people will often be able to see things that you may not have noticed before, and the answers might even surprise you.

You can become educated and talented in anything you set your heart to. Are you confident in giving your passion to the world? If you're not, it's probably because you have yet to develop the skills necessary to have that kind of confidence. Take notice of the strengths you already possess. If you have been engaged in what you're passionate about for a while now, it's likely that you're at least somewhat proficient in it. If this passion is a new discovery, it's likely you still have much to learn. Of course, that's all right—everything can be learned.

Maybe you have a passion for something but you're not quite gifted at it. In my opinion, one great sadness in the world is that this stops a lot of people from pursuing a life of doing what makes them come alive. As my grandparents used to tell me (just like I'm sure every other grandparent said to their grandchildren), "If there's a will, there's a way, Travis." If you really love what you're doing enough, you can find a way to not only become good at it, but to become extraordinary. It usually takes about five to seven key skills to be extraordinary at something, so consider what five to seven key skills you would need to learn in order to be great at this passion. Incredible confidence follows skill, so when you become good at something, you will also become naturally and fearlessly confident. Contemplate what books you can read. What classes or group courses could you take to improve the skills of your passion?

When you have gotten a clear vision on your passions, what you're good at, what the world needs, and how you can be paid for it, you have taken great strides toward discovering your purpose. This kind of inner work may take some deep self-reflection to uncover, but in time, the underlying themes of your purpose will become clear. It's important to do this all with the spirit of play, and to do it all with a sincere, authentic, and thoughtful mind. If you're still unsure what your purpose is, more time and reflection is needed. When you have discovered a path, the rest of this book will guide you to your destination.

PART III:

THE DESTINATION

CHAPTER NINE:

Walking to True North

"All our dreams can come true, if we have the courage to pursue them."
—*Walt Disney*

I. Passion's Great Obstacle

"When I finally discover what my purpose is, and I'm doing what I love, I'll be living the dream!"

I hear this kind of statement all the time, and I used to say it all the time to myself as well. After uncovering my ikigai, I sat on it, only thinking about how great life would be doing what I actually loved for a living. At the time, I never found the courage to actively pursue it, as I did a good job of convincing myself that other people were right, that I could never make any money helping other people live the life of their dreams. Limiting beliefs, unfounded fears, and social conditioning usually stop us before we even get started on our adventure of purpose. Unfortunately, this is where most people who commit to blazing their own trails stop dead in their tracks. We get inspired by the potential of living a life doing what we love; we have a vision about how we want to spend the rest of our lives; and then, one way or another—because of pressures or because we scare ourselves—we allow those dreams to remain unlived, only to haunt us for the rest of our lives, reminders of what could have been.

But discovery of purpose does not come from thinking about what we could be doing with our lives, or thinking about what our purpose is and then abandoning it; it comes from actively showing up into our purpose, showing up in the world, trusting our gut, and doing! Just like in unleashing our spirits of play, we must not stop at thinking about purpose but must instead engage in purpose actively and physically. After three years of thinking about how I could help people the way I wanted to and imagining what life would be like as a result, yet still going to my bartending job day in and day out, I decided that it was time to build some determination and just go for it. I saw no clear destination, but I knew in my gut that I had to listen to my heart, which was telling me that if I started this adventure, the path would make itself clear over time. I knew how important it was for me to follow my core values and my ikigai. I was told over and over again that it was a risky path, and that there was no money in it, but again, I chose to listen to my heart and allowed it to guide me.

Most of us get caught up in asking the wrong questions about what we should do with our lives and wind up doing something that doesn't fulfill us, let alone light our souls on fire. We go through the school system, listen to our parents, coworkers, and friends, all telling us that the journey we're considering just doesn't make good money or is a silly idea. We're told that we might want to think about getting into something different, and we start considering the safer and less-fulfilling path in life. We slowly become conditioned to pursue the money, but here's the thing: when we get caught in that trap and decide to pursue the money first, we tend to blind our-selves to what we could be passionate about while also making money.

When we ask ourselves, "What can I make money doing," there are practically a million answers, but how many of those actually interest you? How many light you up? How many of those options would get you out of bed without your slapping that snooze button over and over? (Mondays don't suck; it's the job that does.) Most importantly, though, how many of these options are your life purpose? Many of us consider the money question first, but when our first question considering a possi-ble career is based on the amount of money we will make, we are mentally closed off to countless other careers that may be unconventional and may not only make us a living, but could also be financially rewarding.

Your first question in order to discover your life purpose should never be, "What can I make money doing?" or even, "What am I interested in that I could make money doing?" Your very first question when imagining a possible career should be: "What am I passionate about?" Get very clear on what that answer is—even if it is a number of different things—and only then ask, "How can I make money doing this?" The pre-supposition of a "how" implies that there is a way—and trust me, through the countless people I've worked with all over the world, there is always a way and there is always the possibility of abundance and prosperity, if you become good enough.

What would you do if money were no object? What would you do if your happiness paid the bills? Forget about the money for a minute. What would you enjoy doing? How would you like to spend the rest of your life? The educational system in our youth is great at creating the belief that it's rare to earn money doing what you love. I don't care what it is that you want to do. I don't care if you want to be an archeologist, a horse trainer, a painter, a musician, or an Olympic bodybuilder—the only thing that is important right now, at this stage, is what would light your life on fire. If you're fixated on money being the most important thing, you will spend your life miserable at some deep level. You will spend your precious time, your one shot at life, doing what you hate doing, so that you can continue to do more of what you hate doing. It's a never-ending cycle of insanity.

You can say that money is the most important thing, but if you believe that, you will end up completely wasting your life. If getting money is what is most important to you, if it's your sole goal in life—as it is with so many people in the world—you will sacrifice anything to get it, even your own happiness. Of course, financial stability is important, and money is a great tool that enables us to live fuller, richer lives that provide us with many great things and experiences. But at what cost do we pursue wealth and monetary gain? So many people view money as the magical treasure at the end of the rainbow, the all-important windfall that will finally give them the happiness, love, admiration, or material things that they've always dreamed of. Most of us will do anything to get it, even sacrifice what is most important to us in the end—our relationships, our health, and our happiness.

Since before we could remember, most of us have been programmed to believe that gaining money at any cost is just the way to live. We see fancy people driving fancy cars, living in fancy houses, buying fancy things, eating fancy food with their fancy friends. We see that and think, if we just had money, we could have those things too and then finally be happy! From our youth we are taught to believe that wealth is the ultimate achievement of someone's life—that if we are rich, we will be happy and respected. How absolutely absurd that is! How ridiculously backward that logic is! If money brings so much happiness, then why are so many people who are obsessed with getting it so unhappy?

Money pays the bills, buys us food, and pays for some fun. But how do you get money for these things? Oftentimes, for far too many people, you work hard at your job—one that statistically you probably hate and feel underpaid for—and work as often as you can to make up the difference. It's a lousy catch-22: spend much of your life working a job you hate, just to keep living a life that makes you so miserable. Please let that settle in for just a minute.

Now, if you are one of the people who thinks money is what is going to make you happy, you are probably forgetting that at the same time that you're paying for your life, you are supposed to be enjoying it, too. What if money were not the currency of the world, and instead your contentment and excitement could be used to provide you with what you need? What if the more excited you were about waking up every morning directly correlated with how wealthy you were? What would happen if you decided to stop living your life based on earning that green paper alone and instead asked yourself, "What do I really enjoy in life? What would make me happy every day? What could make me emotionally rich?"

If you got your electric bill in the mail today and were able to immediately pay it using sheer happiness—because your life brings you contentment, and purpose—what would that feel like? If you wanted to move into your dream house, what else would have to happen in your life to make you happy enough to afford it? I'm sure that doesn't include working at some job where you are unappreciated and undervalued—what would you do if you could work anywhere? What would get you out of bed every morning, before the alarm even went off, with a smile on your face instead of a scowl? How would you fill your time and what would you do to earn happiness? As one of my childhood role models, Scrooge McDuck, said, "No man is poor who can do what he likes to do once in a while!"

What is money worth to you? Are you sacrificing something important in your life to obtain it? Is it worth sacrificing your happiness and not doing all the things you've always dreamed of? If getting money is your sole goal in life, you'll inevitably regret it—if you don't already. Cross boundaries and break the shackles of "normal." Are you willing to sacrifice some things now in order to do what you love in the future? If you must work hard now to pay those bills, then find ways to work more efficiently, and free up your time for other things. Enjoy your day, because this isn't a trial run—this is the big show and a curtain call is coming.

There are three distinct elements of success—passion, persistence, and patience. If you are passionate about what you pursue, it will be easy to be persistent and patient with it. And if you are persistent with it, it will be easy to become a complete master, and you will be able to charge a good amount for your services. It should be of no concern to you whether others are excited about your passion; if you are passionate about it, there is a guarantee that others are as well.

The concept of a work-life balance is driven into our heads as soon as we begin a career. This idea is a slap in the face to anyone who understands the true value of life. Oftentimes, it's something that your employer sends out via email to try to make you a little happier—and thus, more productive—at work. Worst of all, a work-life balance implies that we should have two separate lives—that work and life are two mutually exclusive things. This concept suggests that we must sacrifice an average of forty hours per week at a job we don't like, drive home exhausted, and then—if we're lucky enough—do something that may fulfill us for a brief time. We're told it's normal to sacrifice the meat of our lives so that we may have some semblance of an existence when we're not working. Is that the life you want? Does this concept of a work-life balance send your soul flying? This approach is why people waste away their lives chained in front of the television and to an office desk. A rich life is one that does not necessitate a work-life balance. A truly purposeful life effortlessly merges the two together, like a dance between two lovers.

I have personally worked with people who have had dreams they initially thought were too out there or too far-reaching to be realistic. Our first sessions always start this way. Over time, however, when the mental barriers and limiting beliefs start crumbling down, they start uncovering what their heart is calling them to do. I worked with a man who wanted to become a composer but was told it was impossible, and with a woman who always dreamed of becoming a pre-wedding coach for brides, but wasn't sure if that was a viable or "real" career option. I've worked with everyone—from a mom who wanted to start her own business but didn't "have the time," to a man who wanted to become a shaman and lead people on soul-searching journeys into the desert. My point here is that if we were to address the question of whether it's possible to make money doing these things, it would be easy for these people to convince themselves that it was never going to work out. After all, they've been told their whole lives that it prob-ably wouldn't work, and they didn't get very far as a result. Some got into college debt for a degree they have never used; some, like me, were waiting tables and tending bar at jobs they hated, or working for corporations with values that were the polar opposite of theirs—all because over time they convinced themselves that their big dreams just were not really possible. Because when feasibility is the first thing you consider, you will always come to the conclusion that it's not possible. But by changing that mindset and asking the more powerful and meaningful question, "What do I want?" first, you can work backward from there and figure out your "how." And just like all of these people with their "crazy" dreams—who are now living the dreams that their hearts asked them to live—when you commit to your "what," your "how" comes easy.

Just dream big—I'm talking really big. How you're going to get there should not be your burden yet; it will only limit your imagination in uncovering what's important to you. Your priority at this moment is to only focus on what you want out of your life. Who do you want to become?

II. Living Lucidly

I'm an avid practitioner of lucid dreaming and feel as though lucidity in dreams is a great metaphor for how we can choose to live in our waking lives. Lucidity in dreams, also known as dream yoga in the East, is the awareness that you are in fact dreaming while you are still in your dream. In true mastery of lucid dreaming, you only control yourself within the dream, and allow your subconscious to take care of your surroundings. This practice allows anyone in this lucid state to act out some pretty spectacular things while sleeping. Most people who learn how to lucid dream spend their first moments in lucidity usually flying or having sex with a dream partner; others spend their time on more profound pursuits. By becoming aware within dreams, I was able to add more—not just to my sleeping life, but surprisingly, to my waking life as well. "By waking in your dreams, you can waken to life," psychophysiologist and lucid-dreaming expert Stephen LaBerge said. Within the last ten years, I have passionately practiced and gotten pretty good at this art, and it is an art that I nearly perfected in my midtwenties. One night, I flew all the way to the furthest reaches of the universe only to find a woman wearing a white gown, hidden in a pink fog at the edges of the cosmos. I asked her life's big questions and had some truly life-affirming answers (which I won't spoil, in hopes that you, too, will lucidly fly to the furthest reaches of the cosmos to find your own answers). On another night, I climbed all the way to the top of a snowy mountain peak in the middle of the ocean, and when I looked down upon the world, I gained a new, grand perspective about my place in it. In this moment, I felt small in the grandiose scheme of things, but joyously alive! What incredible perspective that was!

While these lucid dreams were, in fact, nothing more than dreams, they usually meant much more to me. Ask any avid lucid dreamer and they will tell you the insightful meanings they have found by discovering their subconscious through lucidity. After having a lucid dream, I often wondered why we—the people of the world—only allow our wildest fantasies and passions to be lived out under our sheets and with our heads resting on a pillow. Why should we only reserve meaningful lives for our imaginings at night? Why not actually pursue those lives, instead of only dreaming about them?

See, in our waking lives, our visions for ourselves tend to be very limited. We feel constrained in what we can do, what we can accomplish, how much money we can make, or where we can live. We are limited because we are conditioned that we are limited, and our minds don't easily envision beyond the physical limitations of our daily lives. We wait until we fall asleep to think about our fantasies, and only live them out in our deepest dreams. Have you ever woken up from an incredible dream, and all morning you just smiled and smiled? Have you ever woken from a dream and just wished you could fall back asleep to live out the rest of those fantasies? It's a euphoric feeling that we all know.

So what's stopping us from living out those fantasies in real life? Is it money? Is it social pressures? What would happen if

you awoke from an incredible dream where you were a successful artist and then, upon waking up, finally started on your
path of painting? You wouldn't just be excited to fall asleep
and dream; you'd be excited to actually live, to do the things
you had always wanted to do! These things are only a single
question, a single action, or a single dream away. Maybe your
subconscious is actually trying to tell you something—that you
should do these things. You would be, as they say, living the
dream—quite literally living your dreams.

Our limits are only defined by our own imaginations, not
society's expectations, not our work priorities, and not money.
Our dreams should not only be lived when we are asleep; they
should guide us to where we want to go in waking life. They
should be actually lived out in our lives. Why not? What is it
that's stopping you?

Like American author Steven Pressfield once said, "Our job
in this lifetime is not to shape ourselves into some ideal we
imagine we ought to be, but to find out who we already are
and become it." The real adventure of purpose begins when we
free ourselves from what the world expects us to do with our
lives and find the courage to pursue what is already within us.

CHAPTER TEN:

Leaving a Legacy of Purpose

"Carve your name on hearts, not tombstones. A legacy is etched into the minds of others and the stories they share about you."
—*Shannon L. Alder*

I. A Toast to Adventure

If there were a specific trajectory that your life has been taking you, where does it all seem to be pointing you toward? What does it seem like your entire life has been leading up to? What does it look like you were born to do? What do you seem to be in the business of doing? If the universe were shaking you awake, what would it be suggesting that your destiny was? And, most importantly, when you put the pieces of this adventure of purpose together in one sentence, what is your life purpose? While taking in all of your passions and interests, which specific ones stand out to you as encompassing the most meaning? Looking at your talents and skills, which ones do you feel are the most useful and purposeful? A big part of purpose is about making a positive impact on the world, so what does the world need that you would really want to deliver, something you believe in with your entire being? Finally, you have to make a living—so how can you be paid for all of this? The answers to all of these questions can coexist together. What is the single thing they seem to be leading you toward? When the results of what you love, what you're good at, what the world needs, and what you can be paid for all point to a common theme—one that is congruent with your core values—you have uncovered your life's purpose.

These were all questions that I asked myself on one late New Year's Eve after a ten-hour-long bartending shift serving champagne to other people partying a bit too hard to bring in the New Year. I had great talks that night with some patrons about their New Year's resolutions. I held some regulars I knew to a higher standard for their New Year's goals and promised accountability for some to actually follow through with their resolutions. Through the entire night, these conversations were the best and most exciting part of my night. At the time, I had no idea what coaching was, but looking back, I was already coaching behind the bar, and I loved every single second of it.

Throughout my life, I had heard all about what I should be doing; I had listened to people telling me that there was no money in my passions, that I would never make a living having powerful conversations with people. I accepted it all as fact and ignored what my heart was pleading me to do . . . up until that night.

"I don't know how I'm going to do it, but I'm going to guide people into a life of passion and purpose. I want to help the world step out of their limits and into where they dream to be!" I exclaimed while sipping New Year's champagne on my own at 3:00 a.m. I toasted a glass to myself—I didn't care whether or not the world would accept me; all that I cared about was whether I could live with myself if I didn't pursue my dream. I made a sacred pact with myself, a commitment to lean into my purpose and boldly step with courage. In that moment, I felt an incredible relief overcome my entire being, as if I had finally let go of a two-ton backpack that I had been carrying up a giant mountain my entire life. I just knew what I was meant to do with my life—what my calling and my purpose was—and I was going to accept that call to adventure, come hell or high water. I used to have sleepless nights before embarking on my adventure of purpose, but since I let go of that weight and faithfully stepped into my calling on that New Year's Eve, I have not had a sleepless night worrying about what I'm supposed to do with my life. I spent the next two years completely engaged in creating the life I wanted for myself, until almost two years later, through my passion, persistence, and patience, I was able to quit my bartending job and begin living my dream—coaching extraordinary people to step into their power and speaking around the country full-time.

I made another toast to myself: "To purpose and to adventure. It's gonna be a hell of a ride!"

II. Creating a Legacy

What will be left of you long after you are gone? Why are you here, and how will you tell the world and let it echo from the mountaintops? What do you see as your own personal mission, and what if this mission could reverberate through generations? As street artist Banksy said, "They say you die twice. One time when you stop breathing and a second time, a bit later on, when somebody says your name for the last time."

A powerful personal mission is something others will still know about you long after you're gone; it encapsulates your life's purpose in one single sentence. The act of crafting your mission statement not only aids you in gaining even more clarity on what your purpose is, but it also helps you walk with more intent and vigor on your journey. Defining and understanding your purpose in a succinct statement adds so much more meaning and direction to not only your life direction, but it also helps the world better understand and get behind what it is that you have decided to do with your life here. When chaos and challenges emerge and try to throw you off the course of your journey—as they inevitably will try to do—it is easy to get back to true north by recalling your personal mission. A person with their own mission is one who is difficult to stop.

A memorable mission statement should be clear and understandable to anyone who reads it; it should be in alignment with your true self and encapsulate your core values. A truly legendary mission statement should be epic and, most of all, it should be bold, if a bit unconventional. If people don't get behind your mission, that's okay—it's not their mission, it's yours! You may have thought you have discovered true north by now, but your singular mission will be your internal compass, always reminding and guiding you toward the right choices and directions, even when you feel lost on your journey.

An epic and bold mission statement will be epitomized in three parts—what, who, and why. What will you do? Who will you do it for? Why do you want to do it?

Legendary leaders, entrepreneurs, and pilgrims of purpose create epic and bold visions! The true heroes of history and of the future are not afraid to be bigger than life. An epic vision will reflect your core values. A bold vision will make no apologies about wanting to make a dent in the world. They will capture attention from people that need what you are now offering, and due to the adventurous nature of what you're pursuing, it will spark curiosity and interest in the world. Thus, your vision should always speak to your heartbeat, not necessarily to what you believe the world may accept. Never be afraid to stand out from the crowd, because that is where extraordinary things will happen. Who do you notice more in life—those who blend in, or those who boldly go their own way and blaze their own trails?

So, what are you going to achieve? Lay it out there for everyone to understand. Epic visions don't have corporate jargon—nobody cares about that, as it resonates with no one. All that tends to do is make your ego feel a little better about yourself. If you have to explain your mission, you need to make it more accessible. This mission should be universal. Most people you tell about what you are doing should understand it without asking follow-up questions about what you do.

Who will you do this for? Who is your target? Clearly define who it is that you are doing this for. If you can't emphasize who you are seeking to speak to, odds greatly increase that your message will go over the heads of people who want or need what you are offering. Getting focused on exactly who you want to impact speaks directly to your potential audience's hearts, and they will come calling as a result.

Why is what you are doing important for the world to have? The world, either on a small or grand scale, needs what you are going to offer. Why exactly does your potential audience want or need what you have? What is the end result of working with you? What you are seeking to do will change lives in some form—whether the change is dramatic or something smaller is not the point. Always remember that no mission and legacy is too small, as you can impact the world by changing one single life in a positive manner. As long as what you are doing and the manner in which you do it is epic and bold to you, that it is what is important.

Something will happen as a result of your service—there will be some dent in the world—but you must define what that dent is and how big it is going to be. What will happen to the lives of the people who are impacted by your mission, and why is it important that they have what you're pursuing?

Do not feel overwhelmed and scared in thinking that you must to stick with this vision for the rest of your life. You don't have to get this tattooed on your forehead. As the habitual waves of life come and go, as storms present themselves, as you grow, and as life's circumstances unavoidably shift, your priorities may change as well. This is normal and even welcome, so don't resist this. If this happens and you do not change as you move through life's journey, you will not travel as yourself. The river of life is asking you to go into a new place, and the more you fight the current, the more chaos you will bring into your life. As we change through our years, so might our purpose.

The main importance here is that you are clear on your vision today so that you may embark on your own adventure of purpose. Over time, my own vision has evolved into something much richer and more in line with my values, and yours might as well. But my vision was only allowed to grow because I was engaged in my journey.

III. What You'll Learn at Your Own Funeral

Having a personal mission is the most important piece of not only touching lives, leaving an impact, and getting clear on why you're here, but also in handing down a beautiful legacy. Legacies don't just happen, they have to be created, and one of the most powerful ways to define and create your legacy is to get passionately sentimental. You do this by going to your own funeral. Have you ever been to your own funeral? I have . . . and it's an emotional experience. No, I didn't pull a Tom Sawyer, fake my death, and show up at my wake, but I did something unusually powerful once while camping on a secluded oceanside bluff in California: I wrote my own eulogy.

Imagine for a moment that you've just passed away. A bit morbid and melancholy, I know, but there's an important point to be made here. By viewing your passing in an imaginary sense, you have an incredible opportunity. Just like in the old story of Tom Sawyer, one of my favorite books, you are able to view your own funeral. You can look down at your casket, you can hear what people are saying about you, and you can remember your life as it has been lived. All of your loved ones are there—your relatives, friends, and business associates are there too. Everyone you've ever loved or who had meaning in your life is there paying their respects.

It's interesting and emotional to take this imaginary step into the future. From this vantage point, you are able to project how you want others to remember you. When you put your own funeral at the top of your mind, see loved ones sharing stories about your life, and witness your own eulogy, death becomes very clear and very real. And thus, you see how important it is for you to live the life you've always wanted, to live like you really mean it, and to leave a legacy that your friends and family, and even the world, would be proud of.

Reflect for some time in silence on how you've lived your life so far. Get clear on what you've done and where you're heading if you keep going down the road that you have been going on, maintaining the same course. Reflect on how you want to live between now and your death; spend more time here, as this is what's really important. When you look back on your life while on your deathbed, what good will you have done? What kind of greatness do you want to achieve before you finally kick the bucket? What is everyone saying about you during your imaginary funeral, as a result of your living that kind of life? Are they all telling inspiring stories that elicit laughter and joy? Is everyone remembering you for the incredible person you were, all of the good you've done and greatness you've accomplished?

Or is everyone instead talking about the football game they're missing out on, or that they're at your funeral because they feel obligated to be? What do you leave behind to your loved ones? What do you leave behind to the world? Besides the physical contents of your will—besides money, cars, property, and trinkets—what value have you given to those still here? Were you good to the world, someone who gave unconditionally, or were you just a bit of an asshole, someone who took as much as they could and walked all over others to get what they wanted? Did you inspire and encourage others, or did you stifle them? What part of your being remains here long after you're gone? What stories are shared? What good is to be had from your life?

You create your legacy, what you leave behind for the sole reason of benefiting others, during your life. But your legacy doesn't just benefit everyone else; what you do to create that legacy matters to your well-being while you are alive. It's important to base your life and create your legacy on what you want to see in the world. It's not important that you see your entire legacy fulfilled before you pass away, but what is important is that you take action to at least begin to create it. When we start to create our legacy and act in accordance with our ikigai and our deepest core beliefs and values, we are more empowered, confident, fulfilled, and thus much happier for it. We are living on purpose and with purpose. When others see us acting in accordance with our values and beliefs, they are naturally drawn to us.

Choose what you want your legacy to be. Are you creating one right now? If not, how could you begin with what we have discovered so far? Remember that your legacy should always be a labor of love—something you want to do with your heart—that is in accordance with your core values and is your authentic purpose.

What do you want your life to be about? In that same inspired mental place, begin to write out your own eulogy as if someone you love had written it about you. Read it aloud and see how you feel. What did you accomplish? What did you do for the world? How hard did you live? Who did you help? What were the adventures you went on? Just like a real funeral, odds are, if you're doing this right, you'll be crying.

Now that you have your eulogy, it's time to make it a reality and start living like you were dying! What will it take to leave behind that kind of legacy starting today? Ignite that fire in your heart and take the steps to create lasting change! If it is necessary for you to take small steps, take them. Just be sure that you are the living manifestation of the person you want to be remembered as. If you do all of this, if you are an embodiment of your purpose and values, you will have many people—not just your family—celebrating your life at your funeral.

In addition, imagine yourself on your deathbed, right before this funeral of yours. What questions will you be asking about your life? I spend a lot of time talking with the older generation, and I talk to them about what they believe the meaning of life is and often ask what types of things they ask themselves now that they've lived a long life. Most often, I hear things like, "Am I proud of my life?"; "Did I live my own life or someone else's?"; "Did I let my problems get the best of me?"; "Did I take responsibility for my life?"; and "Did I love enough?" These are questions I'm sure I will ask on my deathbed about my own life. What do you believe are the questions you will ask on your deathbed reflecting back on your life? Choosing to start living in alignment with the answers you want is the recipe for living with no regrets. The main idea here is to define your dream life and to begin living in alignment with that life immediately—practically reverse engineering your legacy and dreams.

Go forth, be epic, be bold, and most of all, whether it's in future history books, or what your great-grandchildren tell about you, leave a legacy and story worth writing about.

CHAPTER ELEVEN:

Crossing the Rubicon

"He who has a why to live can bear almost any how."
—Friedrich Nietzsche

I. The Night I Almost Died

On the eve of Marcus' and my twentieth birthdays, we and another friend hopped in my 1977 Volkswagen van and headed south to Carlsbad, a small surf town in San Diego county, on what we planned to be a three-day surf trip to celebrate not only growing another year older, but most importantly, graduating from being teenagers to real, honest-to-goodness men! The plan was to park somewhere secluded and camp in the back of the van for the two nights we would be there, and spend most of the three days surfing as much as we could handle. We arrived in Carlsbad as the sun was setting, parked the van by the beach, and walked down to the water to check what kind of waves we would be surfing the following morning.

The three of us spent a few hours down at the beach, looking at the waves but also sharing stories and having meaningful conversations—talking about our plans for the future and what we wanted to do with the rest of our lives. As the midnight hour came, we resolved to head back to my van to get some sleep before we would wake up at 6:00 a.m. to get on the surf. The waves looked like they were going to be good and we wanted to be on them when the sun came up.

On our walk back from the beach, I noticed in the corner of my eye a four-door black car slowly and quietly pulling up next to us. This struck me as a bit odd—this road was always quiet enough during the daytime, but at night it was pretty much a ghost town. I watched the black car as it stopped next to us, and four men quickly threw open all four doors. As I watched them step out of the car, I noticed that they were all wearing bandanas, concealing their faces with only their eyes showing. Carlsbad is not known for its crime—in fact it's considered a very safe city—so while this alarmed us all, a part of me initially thought it may have been a joke. As the four men walked toward us, they each, at the same time—as if it had been planned and rehearsed dozens of times—pointed four guns at our heads and began screaming at us to give them all our money. This definitely wasn't a joke.

The car rolling up to us, the doors opening, the four men walking with an obvious violent intent toward us and pointing loaded weapons, and the screaming all took no longer than about three or four seconds—three or four seconds that seemed to last for an eternity, but also seemed to have happened in the blink of an eye. After this eternal millisecond, my mind went blank and my memory fades completely. All I can remember is coming to and hearing a profusion of ear-piercing cracks tearing through the predawn silence, violent and bloodthirsty gunshots reverberating through the peacefully empty street. By the time I realized what was even happening, I found myself lying on the sidewalk, unable to move my left leg. I looked around for my brother and friend. In my daze, I noticed that my friend was standing up, already calling the police. Good, he was alive. Wait . . . where was Marcus? As I looked desperately around the street, I saw that my brother was lying in the middle of the street too, only he wasn't moving. *He was dead*, I thought. I was sure of it. "Marcus! Holy shit, Marcus!?" At that moment, I saw him slowly sit up and call my name back. He was alive—sweet relief, he was alive. My heart raced, my pulse was pounding, I was wildly dizzy, but I felt incredible reprieve. I got up to run over to him but was unable to, as I still couldn't move my leg. I looked at it and through my jeans saw a thick smoke rising out of my leg that led back to a bloody wound, and a pool of blood on the sidewalk. Marcus and I had been shot, but we were both alive. This whole experience lasted no more than fifteen seconds; it happened quicker than I could comprehend what was going on, but the memory of that night stayed with us all forever.

I stayed in a cast for many months after that, slowly recuperating from my injury. Family and friends visited the hospital where I spent an entire week, watching the news stories about what had happened to us and slowly realizing the case would go cold and they would never find these four guys. My family and friends were all very somber and frightened about the situation, but I felt something a little different. While sitting in that hospital bed on my first night there, wondering how the night might've gone differently had we all made it back to my van just a minute earlier, I thought of how lucky we were to be alive, to be able to wake up another day, in a hospital bed or not. I began, for the first time in my life, to see just how valuable and precious life was. I saw that life could be taken at any moment, whether we see it coming or not. Hell, all it took to derail a birthday surf trip and end our lives was fifteen measly seconds. We all could have been dead in the blink of an eye. The weight of being gone forever hit me hard, in a way I hadn't considered before. Being a teenager who was just turning twenty, the impending inevitability of death wasn't really something I ever thought about, but on this night, it was something that I felt the magnitude of for the first time in my life. *It could all be gone in a single instant*, I thought.

This single experience, while morbid and sad for most of the people around me, was seen through a different lens in my eyes. Getting shot woke me up quite literally overnight to the fact that life is short and, therefore, invaluably precious. I saw every single day from that point forward as a gift that I could have easily never been able to experience again. I committed myself in that hospital bed to making the rest of my life the best of my life, to making every moment count. Why not live with no regrets, to pursue what I loved and to live a life worth writing about? Getting shot only a few degrees in a different direction could have ended my life, but the realization I had because of that experience in many ways ended up saving my life.

II. The Mistake of Man

No matter how alluring and exciting our missions are to us, we will never get around to making our dreams a reality, unless we can first build the motivation to work toward them. The call to adventure will never go away. For the rest of our lives, our hearts will always remind us of our purpose, calling us to show up powerfully into the life we're destined for, telling us that now it's time to listen. With a culture of inherent pessimism and petty distractions at every turn, learning to be driven toward your dream may be the most important thing you ever do for yourself.

When I work with people in a coaching setting, one of the most important questions I will ask is not how they're going to achieve their dreams, but simply, "Why do you want this?"

Initially on your journey, the question of "why" is much more influential than "how," because your "why," if it is emotionally charged enough, will give you a lifetime's worth of motivation to work toward your dream. Friedrich Nietzsche once said that, "He who has a why to live for can bear almost any how." Along your journey, there will be unavoidable obstacles, challenges, and hardships. Nevertheless, when you get clear on your why, on what it means to you to actually achieve this, you will be much more driven to continue on your journey without turning back (as most do at the first sign of a challenge).

Simply having any "why," however, is not nearly enough. It's more meaningful to get as emotional as you can. A good "why" may inspire you for a day or two, but a truly great "why" will get you to the point that I call "crossing the Rubicon." To cross the Rubicon means to pass the point of no return. This phrase refers to Julius Caesar's army crossing the northern Italian Rubicon River in 49 BC. For some historical context, crossing this river was considered an act of treason, so for Caesar's army, there was no return. They had no choice but to move forward. To build motivation, you must cross your own Rubicon; you must create enough emotional leverage in your heart that you feel like you have no choice but to go boldly into your purpose, like Caesar's army going boldly through the Rubicon River.

There are two forms of motivation—there is "intrinsic motivation" and there is "extrinsic motivation." Extrinsic motivation is driven by external rewards like fame, money, or recognition. Intrinsic motivation is driven by more powerful internal rewards like pride, knowledge, and a sense of accomplishment. Take a moment to think about why, if at all, you're motivated to pursue your life of purpose, right now. Is it internally motivated or externally motivated? When we're extrinsically motivated, we generally don't think about the meaning behind our actions, but instead blindly accept that this mission is what we're supposed to do. This is a very dangerous thing, and will often get you into the same trap of working at a job for the paycheck, perpetually chasing something of no real meaning to you, like a horse chasing a carrot that he never reaches. While working for an extrinsic reward can sometimes increase motivation in the short term, researchers have found that too much extrinsic motivation can actually lead to a decrease in the more powerful intrinsic motivation, which ultimately leads to having no motivation at all.

As we have already seen, it's likely that you're being pressured to take a certain path in life. Are you in this for the money or the fame? If you answered yes, you are extrinsically motivated. Does taking this path in life fill your heart with music? Do you smile at the thought of accomplishing this, not because you have to, but because you really want to? If money wasn't an issue, would you still pursue this? If yes, then intrinsic motivation is what is driving you. This is a powerful thing, and it's important that you learn to harness this power moving forward.

This isn't to say that extrinsic motivation isn't important as well—only that developing motivation intrinsically is significantly more powerful. Set some milestones toward your big dream and every time you reach a milestone, celebrate the success. This, of course, is an example of extrinsic motivation, but when the two types of motivation work as team of sorts, results are more likely. Celebrate your milestones by rewarding yourself in some extrinsic way. Commit to treating yourself to a cigar, a trip, or a night out, whatever works for you; just be sure to celebrate in the spirit of play that excites you.

Now moving on to intrinsic motivation: start asking yourself "why!" Why do you want this? What will achieving this dream and living your purpose contribute to your life? Explore and uncover what the underlying drive to your future actions are. Get crystal clear on this and then see if that drive is in alignment with your core values. If your motives are not in line with your core values, that's all right too—this is all about exploration. Take a step back to uncover something that may be more in line with who you are to recalibrate, readjust, and reposition yourself slightly and do it with a little more purpose this time. How can you tweak your mission and actions to be more in line with your values and your authentic self? Take the time to ask yourself the reason you would want a fulfilling career that you enjoy. What will work like this do for you? How will your life be different as a result? This is the most important thing to start with.

I've found personally, and with those whom I work with, that one of the best ways to cross the Rubicon, to build emotional leverage toward achieving your purpose, and to gain unstoppable intrinsic motivation, is to think about death.

The undeniable fact of life is that we are born, we live, and then, well, we die. There are a fortunate number of us in this world who, between birth and death, don't just live a life, but are truly alive. And by "fortunate," I mean to say that we understand the importance and value of living fully in line with our authentic selves, and we find the means, however necessary, to capture our dreams and live on purpose. The unfortunate live out their days never doing more than thinking about their deepest desires because they make a simple mistake. A mistake that, grievously, most of humankind makes: they take a conscious risk that they will get down to pursuing their dreams and do everything they've ever wanted to do in life later because, at that point, they think, they will have the time.

But the mistake of man is thinking that we have enough time to spare.

It's too often that we hear stories about individuals who are diagnosed with cancer and the doctor tells them they only have a few months to live. They feel undoubtedly saddened. Death is looking at them in the face now. Mortality becomes inevitable. When the end of our lives is so far off, like it seemed for me on the eve of my twentieth birthday, it's near impossible to grasp the concept of being gone forever. But now, in the blink of an eye—whether it's from getting shot, or being told by a doctor that you have a terminal illness—we realize that we will soon be gone. After people come to terms with their departure, they then set out to do all the things they've ever wanted to do. They decide to begin unleashing that spirit of purpose that their hearts have been calling them toward: they travel to the places they've always wanted to go to; they go skydiving for the first time; they climb the tall mountains off in the distance that they've always wondered about; they finally learn how to surf; they say "I love you" to the people who may not have heard it from them enough; they hold their mothers just a little tighter for a little longer; they treat strangers better; they give openly and unconditionally to the homeless; and in these last few months of their lives, they live richly. Most will say, with all their hearts, that it was the best time of their lives. All the nonsense and distractions that have previously overwhelmed their lives quickly become irrelevant.

Each and every one of us are faced with the inevitability of death. It will come, but the truly beautiful thing is that we have the gift of being aware that one day, we will no longer be here. Yes, the knowledge that we will one day die is a gift. We are the only species on Earth, as far as we know, that knows it will someday die. This knowledge is an incredible gift because this is what gives our days meaning. Without it, we would live our lives in a meaningless pattern. When we choose to not reflect on our mortality, we become as lifeless as the species that live without being able to observe this. This knowledge is what should put life in us and get us to live our dreams, to embark on our journeys of true north. However, oftentimes people—like myself—will only actively change their lives when they are faced directly, in a matter-of-fact way, with death. Only when we have a time of death do most of us choose to live. We have the gift of time, but we don't have much of it. Spend that time expressing yourself with the knowledge that, one day, you never will have the ability to do so again—and watch life get fuller as a result.

Death is life's great teacher, but too many of us are excessively preoccupied with trivial pursuits to listen. It's incredibly humbling to realize our fragility, and when we listen fully, our egos begin to diminish, and our souls begin to rise. Listen to that ticking clock and you will allow all the baggage that has been holding you down to come undone. What if you were told that you would die in a couple months' time? How would you choose to live? You don't have to wait for an unfortunate and shocking announcement to decide to live out your dreams and begin to exist fully.

It's far too easy for us to join the rat race, to lose ourselves by always striving for a better tomorrow. We focus on the unimportant things. We sell our spirits for more money so we can buy more things that we don't really need. We tell ourselves that we are only living this way now so we can create a better "someday," but someday, in the deepest recesses of our minds, is never coming and we know it. When we wait to fully live until "someday," that attitude and mindset stays with us for the rest of our lives.

The universe is not conspiring against you. There isn't some cosmic law that's plotting your demise and throwing wrench after wrench in your gears to ensure you just can't get a good deal in life, let alone succeed at anything worthwhile.

No, the universe is not out to get you, but it sure isn't going out of its way to help you either. You must be open to what it has to offer.

Dreamers usually remain dreamers and nothing more because, more often than not, they're waiting for precisely the right time to embark on the journey toward their dreams. *Something just isn't right at the moment. I have to wait until I have more money; I have to wait until the children are out of school; I have to wait until after the holidays.* We tend to do more waiting in our lives than actually living because we're convinced that the time just isn't right to go out there and fulfill our long-held desires. So, we inevitably wait and wait . . . and wait some more, waiting for the "perfect" time to finally put one foot in front of the other. Then when we wait some more, we convince ourselves that something else just isn't right . . . so we wait and wait and blah, blah, blah! By the end of our lives, we usually realize that we spent most of our precious years waiting to start living rather than actually living.

Yes, there will be hiccups and even scrapes and bruises on your journey. There may likely be some figurative broken bones, and you may even get some cracks in your proverbial pottery, but it's your choice, and your choice alone, to either let these events indefinitely put out your fire or use them as some fuel to that fire, as motivation to catapult you further. And you can never convince yourself that you don't have a fire in your belly. You've probably just been putting off igniting the thing for too long because you've kept convincing yourself that "next year will be better." The sobering news is that the timing will never be just perfect—so you must take the leap.

Imagine that your bank credits your account every single morning with $86,400. This sounds pretty amazing to you, I'm sure. What a great bank, to just give you all that money! Of course, as with any bank, the money comes with a couple of conditions. The first is that every night at midnight, any unspent remaining money is removed from your account. It is stripped away, gone forever, never to be seen again. Tough luck if you didn't spend it. If you didn't use it, you lose it. The second catch is that at any moment this bank can take all the money from your account, with no warning at all, and forever stop giving it you. I guess that's fair—after all, the money is a gift every day to you anyway. What would you do with this money day to day? Year to year?

I bet you wish you had a bank like this, but the fact is that each and every one of us already has a similar account; but each day we are given something more valuable than money. Even the richest people in the world would tell you that money has very little to do with being truly wealthy. A rich life is not made valuable because of how you spend your money; it is made valuable by how you spend your time. So, our bank credits us not with money, but with a more precious commodity: time. Every morning when you wake up, you are given the gift 86,400 seconds to spend, and every night, whatever you don't use for a good purpose, invest wisely, or have a little fun with, is lost forever, stripped away and never to be seen again—so be sure to not waste it!

After my brother and I went through that horrifying night in Carlsbad, each thinking the other was dead, I began to look at my time left in terms of a dwindling bank account. When I look at my choices of how to spend my time through the metaphor of material dollars—either burning through it and wasting it away or investing it wisely by putting it toward a good use—I make sure to do my best to spend that "money" on something important to me. I'm able to choose wisely and clearly what to do with that time and appreciate how important and valuable my time here on Earth actually is.

Time is fleeting and, therefore, precious. It's not that life is too short; it's just that we wait too long to start living. Sit down and have a talk with anyone who's been diagnosed with a terminal illness or who is in their golden years, and they will tell you that none of the extrinsic motivations matter. The realization that death is looming suddenly helps us get clear on what really matters in life. The thing is, you don't have to wait until you're on your deathbed to get clear on that—you can gain that knowledge now. Knowing that we will die isn't a bad thing; it's a good thing. We just have to be aware of it now and choose to live the kind of life that matters to us. It is empowering to know how much of a positive impact we can make during our lives.

CHAPTER TWELVE:

Koa, the Warrior's Spirit

"The cave you fear to enter holds the treasure you seek."
—Joseph Campbell

I. Hawaii

Flights to Hawaii are something special. Usually the flight attendants will adorn you with leis. The tropical, carefree mood is set long before you even set foot on the islands. Marcus and I were flying to Hawaii the year after we both graduated high school to spend a week crossing off a bucket-list item—surf the north shore of Oahu. We were definitely excited, spending the flight sipping our pineapple, orange, and guava juice mocktails, dreaming about the amazing waves we were going to ride when we landed. We had spent our entire surfing lives catching Southern California swells, and that entire time, the north shore was calling our names. We would tear out pictures of the Hawaiian waves from any surf magazine we could lay our paws on and hang them up in our room.

Our hotel was on the south shore of Oahu, in a little beach town of Honolulu—the world-famous Waikiki. We threw our bags on our beds, put on our board shorts, waxed up our surf-boards, and ran out of the hotel doors, barefoot and shirtless, to Waikiki beach. This being the south shore of Oahu, we weren't expecting particularly epic waves, or even decent-sized waves—nothing like the waves we expected to find on the north shore. But we were finally in Hawaii and we were going to be damned if we had to wait until tomorrow morning to surf. *Hawaii is Hawaii; I'm not about to start getting picky*, I thought.

Marcus and I paddled out into the warm Hawaiian water to the lineup of one- to two-foot faces. Hardly anything to write home about, but surfing in new waters was a beautiful and adventurous experience for us both. We shared waves back and forth for hours, eventually watching a Hawaiian luau and fire show from the water. It was happening on the beach and was complete with one of the most glorious sunsets from the water. The end to a beautiful night and talk of tomorrow's drive to the north shore had us stoked.

The north shore is a magical and mythical place, especially for a surfer. There's an otherworldly feeling about standing on the shore of legendary surf breaks like Banzai Pipeline and feel-ing the vibrations in the sand from two tons of water while twenty-foot faces crash down onto the razor-sharp reef. It's almost as if you're in the presence of Neptune himself, as if he's manifesting the entire ocean into a single, bigger-than-life wave to show you not only the beauty of his domain, but also the power of the sea.

A place like Pipeline is fun to pay witness to, in a dra-matic sort of way, but it's something else entirely to paddle into. Surfers at Banzai Pipeline are a rare breed, embracing their fear and dancing elegantly with the full power of the ocean crashing down on the razor-sharp reef. If Neptune were challenging these people, they embraced the challenge with the spirit of a warrior, playing full-out and enjoying the ride along the way. Marcus and I watched these legendary waves for a couple of hours before deciding to play it a bit safer—and a little less insane—going west on the road to a lesser-known but still powerful surf break known as Chun's Reef. Chun's Reef is known as a long, crumbling wave, but make no mistake: when the winter swells arrive, they manifest some very large and powerful surf. On this Hawaiian autumnal day, there was a large and powerful swell in the water.

We threw on our trunks, waxed up our boards, and jumped straight in the water. Finally, we were going to be surfing the world's famous north shore of Hawaii. Sure, it wasn't a place like Pipeline or Waimea Bay—those kinds of waves were so far beyond our abilities, we'd be insane to even try—but we were surfing the north shore, baby . . . and we were excited. The paddle out to the main break was all smiles and laughter between the two of us until we made it out past the breaking waves and sat on our boards.

Once I got to a position of waiting for a wave, the reality set in. Yes, I was on the north shore, and yes, that was an amazing thing, but the waves on the north shore of Hawaii were completely different animals from the ones I was used to back home. The surf here had a different, much larger power. The energy was almost palpable. Neptune was talking to me, and he was telling me that even though I hadn't paddled into Pipeline, I was still in way over my head. I had only been surfing for just over two years, and here I was, watching ten-foot monsters rise out of the deep blue depths of the water, violently crashing down into reef that was too sharp to even walk on, spitting air out of the eye of the barrel in a shotgun fashion, booming with the fury of a thunderstorm.

I was terrified.

In the middle of my terror, a group of waves rose up over the horizon. While I decided to wait this set out to catch my breath and "grow a pair," I watched Marcus paddle into his first wave. From outside, I saw him drop in, and then saw no more of him from my vantage point. I was sure he had a mouthful of reef to eat for breakfast. The wave went on and on for what seemed like ages. About twenty seconds passed and I started growing more worried, as I hadn't seen him resurface. Just at that moment, I watched him effortlessly pull out of the back of the wave some hundred yards down.

"Oh my Goooooood, did you see that?" he shouted at me.

I was in awe; that may have been the largest and longest ride I had ever seen him catch. I was impressed, but as brothers are—especially at that age—I had to one-up him. As the next set of waves rolled over the horizon, I swallowed nervously, lay on my board, puffed out my chest, and began to paddle for the first wave. *It's now or never, Travis*, I thought. *Just go!*

With my mind focused on not getting a mouthful of coral, this ten-foot show of power began to lift me up. I paddled as hard as my arms could keep up with. Higher and higher the wave lifted me up, until I could see the vibrant colors of the coral reef through the clear, tropical water. The juxtaposition of my awe and terror struck me. The wave began to pitch, getting ready to slam tons of raw, natural power into the razor reef. With my eyes intently looking at where I didn't want to be, I timidly popped to my feet to slide down the face of the wave. Only by then, it was too late. The lip of the wave grabbed hold of my body with the kind of power that a three-hundred-pound NFL linebacker would be jealous of.

Weightless and flying toward the reef, I prepared myself for the inevitable. This was going to be bad . . . really bad. As if Neptune were introducing me to the north shore by showcasing its incredible power, the wave dumped me straight down, slamming my body violently on a floor of razor-sharp edges. I tumbled underwater a handful of times, my hands wildly grasping for the surface, whichever direction that was in. The slam on the water's surface had already knocked all the wind out of me. Frantically trying to reach air was futile, as another wave crashed over me, throwing my body across the reef once more. This time, I felt it, too. I put my feet on the razor reef and bounced up to the surface. A quick half gasp of air before the next wave of the set pummeled me back down and across the seafloor. By this time, I was convinced it was a fight for my life. I swam back up and saw another wave headed right toward me, ready to crash in front of me. Through my daze, I realized that it looked like I had time to swim parallel to the shore so as to avoid the crashing wave and make it to the softer shoulder of the oncoming wave. I swam for my life, the wave moving quickly toward me. And just in time, as if Neptune knew I had no more in me, I made it to the shoulder. I breathed a few heavy breaths and pulled my leash to grab my board and paddle in toward shore before I got pummeled again.

In the time it took me to catch my breath, I thought of how good it would feel to lie on the sand, safe. But, strangely, at the same time, I thought of the regret I would surely feel if I gave up after only one try. How often would I ever get this chance again? *I'll feel like a coward forever*, I thought. *I'll never forgive myself if I don't at least get one more.* I had caught my breath. I looked at my body and noticed that it was only marginally bruised, my ego surely more so. I moved my limbs . . . Nothing was broken. Was this a sign? I took it as one and paddled back out into the lineup, joining Marcus. On the way out, I recalled a quote pinned to my bedroom wall, from one of the true pioneers of big-wave surfing in Hawaii, Buzzy Trent: "Waves are not measured in feet and inches, they are measured in increments of fear." Yeah, I was scared, Buzzy, but on that day, I was committed to not letting that fear define me.

A very tan Hawaiian native on a nine-foot longboard paddled by me, slowing down enough so that I could keep up with him on my much shorter board.

"Nasty, bruddah. You okay?"

Sheepishly, I nodded my head.

"You too scared, bruddah. Relax. Breeeeeathe. See, like dis." He illustrated a deep breath in and out.

I followed his example, not really sure what he was getting at. *Crazy kook*, I thought, immediately embarrassed at myself for judging this man, who had a bigger smile than I did at the time.

"You too scared," he repeated. "*Koa*, haole. You gotta be like a warrior."

A word stuck out to me. "Koa?" I asked.

"Hawaiian, haole. Means fierce—be brave, be bold, be fearless. Koa." A long pause as we paddled out together. The silence between us, I felt, was understood. I was listening intently.

"Breathe, bruddah. Just breathe. Relax, but be fierce. Koa."

Again, to save my energy, I nodded my head as I paddled back out to sit next to Marcus. After he made sure I was all right, at least physically, we sat in silence.

There was a long time for reflection before the next set of waves greeted us over the horizon. I thought about regret, I thought about going home empty-handed, and I thought about koa. I paddled for the first wave, putting everything I had into each stroke. I puffed up my chest just a little higher than before. I chose to look at this approaching wave not with a sense of dread, but with a sense of spirit. It was now or never. I chose to replace thoughts of me being ravished on the reef again with thoughts of playful fun—not being thrown by the wave, but dancing with the wave.

The wave approached. Twelve feet that seemed like twenty and that were ready to throw me over the razor reef.

Koa! I thought it like an incantation, setting my intention to approach this ride embracing courage, not fear. The wave picked me up with the same intensity as the last one. I noticed the razor-sharp reef directly below me. I embraced the courage—I slowed down my breathing, focused on the beauty of the ride instead of the sheer terror that my mind was screaming at me to notice, and smoothly jumped to my feet. Turning right to avoid the breaking lip, I now came face to face with it. My mind went to being thrown across the sharp reef.

Still scared, I instead smiled.

Koa.

Breathe . . .

I ducked just under the throwing lip, wanting to close my eyes to brace for impact, but keeping them open instead, to embrace the dance. The lip pitched over my head. Now I found myself deep inside the eye of the wave. In the heart of the ocean. "The green room," as it's known to surfers. Except this view was inside the crystal-blue eye of the wave. I stood with my bare feet on my board, sliding over crystal water, two feet above reef that might as well have been painted by the universe's best artist. Raccoon butterflyfish swam underneath and in front of my board. I looked out of the breaking barrel, to the tropical trees and sands. Time slowed down. I was in paradise; I was loving life. The wave spit me out to the shoulder with an enormous force, as I pulled out and paddled back into the lineup for another ride. It was time to dance with the ocean again.

Besides the sheer fun, euphoria, and exhilaration of riding waves, what surfing teaches me about life is just as beautiful . . . and has taken me close to a decade to truly discover. To be a great surfer, we must learn not to be scared and anxious, but rather calm and focused—even in the biggest and scariest surf. Anxiousness and fear lead to falling. Calmness and focus lead to beautiful memories with the waves. See, great surfing is not about controlling your path on the wave, but rather about allowing the wave to guide you. There's a balance here, and when that balance achieved, it's like a dance. This is flow. Life is like surfing—there's a wave showing our own unique way; we just have to open our hearts and learn to dance with it.

On that day out on the north shore, I learned something greater than how to surf with ease. I learned how to live with ease, how to embrace fear and dance with the wave of life. I learned that if you don't ever feel fear in your life, you are either dead or not living big enough. Fear is not something to run away from. By running away, we not only allow that fear to dictate the direction of our lives, but we allow it to make us paddle in toward shore with our tail between our legs, always wondering, "What if?"

It's important instead to fully embrace that fear, to embrace the spirit of koa like a fierce warrior and rise above fear.

II. Feeding Your Wolf

My favorite kind of fear is the fear of rejection, and what others will think of us when we choose to paddle into life's big waves. People, friends, and even some family will tell us, before we begin our journey toward our dreams, that it's "probably not realistic." We might hear questions like, "Are you crazy?"

It's not really that the world—especially your friends and family—doesn't want you to succeed; it's just that they don't want to see you fail. They don't want you to take that leap in case you fall, never mind if you fly. They're scared for you, and that's justifiable because they've been told many of the same things throughout their lives and were filled with the same unfounded fears that they're instilling in you now. This is a peculiarly noble thought in a way—just not one that's conducive to growth, let alone an enriched life of passion and purpose. Everyone thinks they're doing you a service by saving you from yourself and that great big, bad, mean world, but what they likely don't know is what every successful person *does* know—that in order to reach our dreams, we must be open and willing to fail and fall. Scraped knees, broken hearts, and scratches from getting dragged across life's sharp reefs are good; they mean you've stood for something extraordinary—that you sought to grow, to undertake something big, to catch an epic wave, to learn and develop. To be robbed of that is to be robbed of the opportunity to blossom. Sure, our friends and family try to protect us and shield us from that great big scary world. They would hate to see us stumble, but in trying to shield us, they are inevitably—though almost never purposefully—preventing us from accomplishing all sorts of magnificent wonders. The rest of the world doesn't understand that to us, the end reward is probably worth a scraped knee or two.

As human beings, and especially in our Western culture, we are habituated to resisting change, to shying away from anything that we are not directly accustomed to, even if they're the smallest of changes. We fight change because throughout our lives, we're told that change is scary and that it's best to stay home and watch people live extraordinary lives on the television rather than to actually seek those kinds of lives for ourselves. Of course we're scared—who the hell wouldn't be? It's normal to feel this way. We tend to be petrified of the journey that is calling to us because those that surround us on a daily basis—the media, our society, and our culture—have conditioned us to be scared, even if it means pursuing something we're interested in.

But here's the truth about fear: more often than not, it's nothing more than an unfounded concept in our imaginations, and one that prevents us from living fully. We've grown up to resist change so much that we never engage ourselves in exploration, and by never pursuing change, we never understand the deep growth that it can bring into our lives. The basis for all fear is ignorance of something, and that is why you will hear those who do not seek growth in their lives, who never pursue their passions, speak of how scary they think the journey of growth is. They say this because they simply don't understand it. Nevertheless, those who take on their passions—and life, for that matter—soon come to the realization that fear is nothing more than a construct that they created in their minds and that prevented them from truly coming alive. If you sat down to have coffee with anyone who actually went out and journeyed toward their dreams, and asked them what to do, they would never tell you to run from your fear; they would tell you that fear is something you should face head on, like a warrior going to battle to slay the mighty dragon that's kept the village in a constant state of fear. Because if you don't take control of your fears, your fears will assuredly take control of you. Choosing not to run from your own life, in effect, allows life to run to you. When you change your thinking about fear, you begin to change your entire world.

It's such a sadness to see so many people living well below their potential because they allow this learned and unfounded fear to get in the way of where they aspire to be. People don't drop into the wave of their lives because they're scared of falling. What would happen if they made the drop? What seems to be an insurmountable mountain will become a simple molehill if we only have the courage to approach it. Too often, we use that dirty feeling of fear as a kind of excuse, an excuse to not do something meaningful with our lives. We tell ourselves over and over that it's okay, that it's just a part of life. When it comes down to it, if asked, most of us aren't sure why accomplishing something so great is that scary or that difficult in the first place! We are exceptionally good at allowing the environments around us to condition us, to mold us, and so, we acquire this fear over the course of our lives, whether it's real or not.

Fear is necessary for survival, yes. It's an evolutionary trait that has kept our species around for hundreds of thousands of years. Fear is a response that advises us to stay safe. That's a good thing, of course, but too much of a good thing is never very good at all. As this fear helps us survive, however, we are hardwired to feel similarly during any new and unexplored situations, no matter how nonthreatening they actually are. Anything new to us will make our fight-or-flight instincts kick in, and, as such, our adrenaline mixes up our minds, which then confuses something we should actually fear with anything new at all, and this is where the problem arises. The emotional response is the same: run! A threat should be avoided. Potential for growth, however, should be approached. As our minds mix these two things up, it becomes easier to sit in our fear and remain stagnant as a consequence.

Too much fear is not something we are born with, but rather something we learn over time. If people tell us over and over again that something is impossible, that we'll surely fail, or that the odds just aren't in our favor, we actually start believing them, whether the facts are there or not. If one person says that we're just not good enough, we begin to believe it, even if countless others do believe in us. When we hear these limiting thoughts thrown at us enough times, over and over again, we begin to accept them as facts.

Fear is the single mindset that will prevent most of us, even those on our journeys of purpose, from being fully engaged in our lives. When it comes down to it, after all is said and done, it's not money, time, or circumstances that prevent most of us from living fully—it's that we're scared to journey into the unknown. We're good at projecting worst-case scenarios on everything. We convince ourselves in the farthest corners of our brain that the worst—no matter how unlikely—will inevitably happen to us. But the truth is, we never really know for sure, because we don't ever decide to take the leap and discover it for ourselves. We literally let fear run our lives, without ever testing to see if the journey forward is something we actually should fear.

Fear is the most prominent thing that is limiting your highest potential. If you're allowing this fear to control your life, you're living in an extremely limited reality—one that you think is so important and you're so afraid to lose. But when you actually test those fears and ultimately overcome them, you will find that you were only allowing your fears to keep you living this limited life and you will wonder to yourself, "What the hell took me so long?"

You've already decided where you want to go. You already have an idea of some path that you'd like to take. If you choose not to embark on this quest, you will spend the rest of your life regretful, wondering what life would have been like if you had only pursued your purpose. Worrying about the outcome will only change your strength to deal with the challenge at hand; it will never change the outcome. It's well-known that about 99 percent of our fears never come true anyway, so letting the fear of what could happen overcome you and worrying about what could go wrong is essentially stressing yourself out over a myth that you keep telling yourself.

Fear oftentimes transcends into anxiety, because that fear begins to eat at us. Anxiety is usually caused by two things—attachment to the unnecessary and avoidance of the necessary. Our purpose is necessary to our souls; our fears are unnecessary attachments that we hold on to. Continuing to avoid engagement in our purpose will only cause more anxiety for us throughout our lives, and the more we dissociate ourselves from our purpose, the more we associate ourselves with our unfounded fears and the more anxiety we will inevitably encounter.

Our hearts are calling us toward something extraordinary. We have discovered what we want the rest of our lives to be about, and yet we choose to wait, to not take action just yet. This decision to wait is a fear-oriented mindset. We know that "someday" is just an excuse we keep telling ourselves so that we can face ourselves in the mirror the next morning after waking up in a cold sweat, wondering where all of our years went. If you keep waiting until someday, you'll be waiting for the rest of your life. With that "someday" attitude, you will always convince yourself that the time will never be just right; the stars will never be neatly aligned for you to begin your journey of purpose. Your soul will only become eaten up by thoughts of what could've been if you allow this "someday" mentality to control you. If you've been anxious most of your life, I'm willing to bet that it has a lot to do with ignoring your inner compass, or at least avoiding some circumstance in life. In doing so, you are allowing fear to control you. You must take the steps towards the direction your inner compass is calling you to travel, and if you choose to not take action, you allow fear to run your life. In order to live fully, you must abolish the "someday" mentality and start your journey today.

I'm sure you can imagine by now that living a life this way—forever waiting for things to be perfect, and allowing fear to control your life rather than you controlling your own life—can cause not only anxiety but an immense amount of heartache and internal pain. We avoid being engaged in what our hearts are calling us to do and we allow unfounded, untested fears to dictate our destinies. Even before you take the leap, it's important for you to understand how fear works, where it comes from, and what to do about it so you can fully abolish it.

There's an old Native American story that I love where a child asks an elder what she'd done in her life to become so respected and wise. She told the young boy that she had two wolves battling for control inside her heart—there was a wolf of hate and a wolf of love. The wolf of hate was fearful, angry, and resentful, while the wolf of love was loving, compassionate, and peaceful. The child asked the elder which wolf would win the fight, to which the elder responded, "The one I choose to feed."

Hypothetically, you have a wolf of love and a wolf of hate in your own heart. Our wolf of hate usually manifests itself in the form of fear, a fear that's been part of our beings since we were cavemen. You can call it whatever you want—inner chatter, lizard brain, the caveman brain, the survival brain, or the monkey mind, as Zen Buddhists call it—the point is that fear is what has helped our species survive for hundreds of thousands of years. It has done a good job and it will continue to do a good job; it's just that the fear has overstepped its bounds and is not helping us thrive. The other part of our beings, that wolf of love, can usually manifest itself in the form of faith. This part of our beings cultivates spiritual experiences, creativity, success, and euphoria. Again, call it what you like—the higher self, higher consciousness, the right brain, whatever. That inner fear has helped us survive, but exactly what good is surviving if we're not thriving? This is where our wolf of love comes in, the part of our beings and brains that is there to help us thrive, to accomplish wonders, and to guide us toward our dreams. We need both parts of this thinking; however, as the wolf of hate is more chaotic, it will too often scream over our wolf of love instead of learning to live in harmony with it.

To help tame this wolf of hate, we mustn't cage it per se, and we certainly shouldn't ignore it, but it is useful to try to have a kind of conversation with it. We must seek to understand what our wolf of hate is trying to scream at us, so that we can quell its concerns. Having this kind of conversation between these two proverbial wolves ensures that our thinking is not constantly at war, but rather in harmony. When we feed the wolf of hate, our minds become feral and out of control; but over time, we can train the wolf of hate to socialize with us, even in a productive way. In the same way, we will learn to train our wolf of hate.

By exploring your fears and understanding this wolf of hate, you will notice a few things start to happen. You will learn about your fears, becoming less ignorant of what you're scared of, so that you have a better understanding of where your fears are coming from and ultimately find that they may be unfounded. This realization causes less resistance in your inner self. You will become more energized in life and will spend more time focusing on possibility, whereas before you would have been consumed by your fear. By working with this primitive wolf, you will notice less of that screaming-monkey thought pattern in your head, and you will find more inner peace. With less resistance, more energy, and more peace, your mind will open up to finding possibilities that you haven't been able to see, rather than finding problems where there previously were none.

The best way to understand and overcome your fears is to imagine them as if they were yourself as a scared child and talk with them. How did you like to be talked to when you were a small child? Probably with patience and kindness. In the same way you would talk with a child, talk with your fears. And when you find yourself working to quell these fears and answering these questions, imagine that you are here to protect that little child self of yours, that you are helping this child understand their fears and concerns. Ask questions like a wise sage and answer these questions as you would when you were a little child who wanted to feel safe, slowly calming the irrational wolf of hate.

Begin to have a conversation with that inner child. Write down the questions you want to ask that child. Help stabilize the fears that this child has by asking, "What are you scared of? What are you worried about?" Ask, and then keep your heart and mind open for the answers. Write down the answers that your inner child is telling you. Write it all down, even if it sounds ridiculous. Listen to the responses and put them on paper. Write the answers the same way your inner child is telling them to you.

From the perspective of our wiser wolf of love, talk with that child, tell them why they don't need to be afraid anymore. Whenever you feel fear screaming over your inner mind, sit down and have a conversation with it. Discover where the fear is coming from and find a way to calm and overcome it. What is your wolf of hate screaming at you? What are your fears and concerns? Why have you been held back? Why have you not been authentically you? Why not surrender? Is this a rational or irrational fear? Realistically, what is the worst thing that could happen? In the slight chance that the worst thing does happen, how can you be prepared for it so that you may ease your mind? Instead of focusing on what could go wrong, ask yourself, what could go right? Finally, ask yourself: What is your first step toward testing this fear?

Unfounded fear is something that you learned as you grew older. Reflect for a moment on the happiest day of your childhood. Do you remember what you wanted to become? What was it that actually stopped you from becoming that? Was it the feeling of not being good enough? Consider how valid that fear was. Now, imagine your present self, going back to that exact time in your life when you were a child. Hold that little version of you close. How would you give that child a piece of wisdom and advice on how you could have battled that fear and created that future for yourself? That fear is meaningless now, isn't it? In that same way, it's likely that the current fear you're facing is meaningless. Tell your younger self how insignificant that fear was, how all it did was prevent you from who you were destined to become.

Now imagine yourself about thirty or forty years later. What does that version of you look like? What are you wearing? How are you carrying yourself through the world? Imagine that that older and wiser version of you is hugging the you of now, telling you that everything is going to be okay. What would that future self tell you about fear and living your dreams? Is choosing to conquer your fears and living your life of purpose worth it to this older version of you? Treat what is expected of you like you did when you were a kid, when you had yet to become jaded from misleading fear.

It's a safe bet that many of these fears have been getting to you for a long time, sucking away at your childlike spirit. Whether you consciously realize it or not, slowly and surely, these fears are preventing you from living a life of passion and doing what you have been dreaming of. These fears are oftentimes nothing more than deceptive fabrications and simply untrue stories unconsciously created by the wolf of hate, which we allow to run free without letting our wolf of love put it in its place. Too often these fears and stories are not valid and hold no weight under the slightest scrutiny; therefore, it's important to take a closer look, to think through and test these fears. If we don't, we fall trap to allowing these fears to grow like a cancer to our spirits. No matter how unfounded these fears are, we eventually start believing them. We sabotage ourselves, and we live our lives wishing we had the courage to pursue a life worth living when the fear was never even real in the first place. Your journey of purpose is much bigger than your wolf of hate that is telling you it's not safe to pursue. Your fears will do their best to keep you from following your paradise, and if you don't sit down and have a conversation with them, they will only grow until they overcome your very being and put you in emotional chains.

If the foundation of fear is ignorance of the unknown, the best way to overcome the fear is to simply make the unknown a little less unknown. For example, if your purpose—like a previous client of mine—is to become a photographer shooting native tribes of the world, but you don't even know how a camera works, you can slowly test that fear by taking a small photography course. After you've taken the course—or maybe even after a few classes—you'd like to start talking to professional photographers and see what they're doing. Afterward, you can expand that comfort zone and test that fear even further by shooting documentary-style photos near home to build up your portfolio. Then, once your comfort zone is expanded further, you might want to travel to the Amazon to shoot your first tribe. It's all about taking steps and getting familiar with the unfamiliar, to make your purpose less mysterious than it was. Fear is lost through confidence and courage; and confidence and courage are gained through action. When you gain confidence, you begin to see the world differently, and when you see the world differently, you are more empowered to create the kind of results that looked impossible before. This is what happens when you feed your wolf of love: your fears become fairy tales and your dreams become tangible.

III. Life Outside the Comfort Zone

Do you want adventure? Do you want a life of excitement that will ignite interesting stories that you can share with your kids one day? You can have that; you just can't have it while sitting cozy in your comfort zone. Spending your life never pushing the boundaries of what makes you uncomfortable will inevitably lead to you feel stuck in a perpetual state of boredom because you're not trying new things. And hey, life should not be a bore.

Of course, the biggest reason we will not try new things is the fear and anxiety that change will cause us. We're anxious when trying something new, and maybe scared of what people will think of us when we're doing something we've never done before—and we let that mental stumbling block get in our way so that we never even try. We don't want others to think of us as weirdos, crazy, or failures. How profoundly heartbreaking that is, that so many people want to try new things and sacrifice doing them for an unfounded fear of what people will think of them. There's a reason it's called the comfort zone. It's comfortable because you know exactly what's going to happen when you're in it. There are no surprises here, and it's relatively safe. Where's the fun in that? Where's the spirit of adventure? Leaving this area of comfort can be scary because in the back of your head, you think something could go wrong, and if you venture too far out, you could—*gasp*—fail. At least that's what that screaming monkey is telling you. Guess what, though? Even with the slight chance that you do fail, you will always gain something very valuable.

Stop and think about some of the most magnetic and interesting people in your life. I'm willing to bet that they have just a brush of what others might call "crazy" within them. They like to step out into the world, try new things with little regard for what others may think of them, and if they fail, they fail. They move on—and usually they're more interesting and exciting to be around for having tried! They've usually lived very fully and are easy to talk to because they've experienced a lot that life has to offer. If people laugh at them, they don't take it personally, and they can even laugh with them. There's a certain charm to that. Mistakes will be made. That's good . . . You grow that way!

In most worst-case scenarios, you faced your dreaded fear and more than likely learned that that fear was groundless and wasn't that scary. In fact, stepping into that fear was probably sort of exciting—it made you feel alive, didn't it? By stepping out of your comfort zone, you also did something very important. You stretched it out just a little bit farther and wider, and by stretching your comfort zone, you are openly allowing yourself to become a part of some incredible new things—things you maybe thought you were too scared to take part in! It takes practice to get good at leaving your comfort zone.

We really do think too much sometimes—this is that inner wolf of hate convincing us that what could go wrong will go wrong. The remedy for this is to quit focusing so much on what will happen when you do something that is new and out of your comfort zone. Instead, focus on the actual activity itself. Relish the moment, not in the result. Be mindful of what is happening right now and enjoy yourself. Live in the moment, right now, not for what might happen in the future—even seconds from now. Relinquish control of what may happen, and if you do this correctly, you will have no stress over it, not even a bit. And even if things do go badly (and they almost never do), it doesn't matter, because you aren't focused on the outcome. If you don't get the desired result, no big deal; you put no stock in it. If you don't do anything, you won't get what you want either. But only by going for it do you actually grow.

The key is to dive into your fear and to stretch your comfort zone in some way every day. Find something to do that will get you closer to your dream, or some new way to leave your comfort zone that will get you closer to your purpose. I'm not saying you need to jump off a cliff into shark-infested waters to tame that wolf of hate, but it's important to find some small way to stretch yourself every day so that it's put in its place. The idea is to stretch your comfort zone every day so that it becomes larger and wider, and you'll eventually get lost outside of it, living much more fully and closer to your purpose! When you stretch yourself that way, your comfort zone becomes so large that you open yourself up to new opportunities, new experiences, and you learn so much more—not only about the world, but about yourself as well.

Do not focus on trying to be unafraid; remember that you are a human being and literally anyone with a pulse will be scared, especially when embarking on such an epic quest. The only people who aren't scared are either six feet under or are not living large. Instead, commit yourself to taking action in the face of fear, one step at a time. Step into your fear to test and overcome it. Courage is a lot like a muscle. We don't go to the gym and start lifting the heavy weights right away; we pick up the smaller weights until our muscles are ready to go a little bigger. Eventually, we build up enough strength to lift with the big guys. Developing courage is the same way, so start by working out your courage muscles with small steps. If you do something every day that scares you, even a small thing, you will grow exponentially. Maybe that small thing is scary to you right now, but after a while, you'll look back and wonder why it prevented you from so much, and you'll be able to test your biggest fears without even flinching.

When testing your fears so consistently, you are learning to become comfortable with being uncomfortable. We are only ever confined by the prison that we build ourselves, and our lives are limited by the safety and security of our comfort zones. We grow to become most courageous in life by expanding this comfort zone. By choosing to be uncomfortable, we challenge and scrutinize our fears, and after a while, what previously scared us isn't so scary anymore. Feel that fear, taste it, feel that discomfort, let it consume you for a moment, understand why you're scared and then . . . step into it. This is how you cultivate true courage and embrace koa, the true warrior's spirit. You don't have to go all in right away—just get your feet wet in the river of life. Staying in your comfort zone only creates more fear. The more you let your fear keep your life confined to your comfort zone, the more that fear spreads. Eventually, fear is what starts running your life, not you. Now that's something truly scary. Like the heroes of the great stories, if you choose not to explore your limits, you will never know just how far you are capable of going. When you decide to never test and own your fears, you allow your fears to own you, because seeking safety in avoidance of fear is the enemy of all success.

IV. The Hero's Journey

Think of any great adventure story, from Homer's *The Odyssey* to J. R. R. Tolkien's *The Lord of the Rings*. In all of these extraordinary stories of triumph, our hero chooses to go boldly out into the unknown. They do this because their heart is calling them to it. Are they scared? Of course, they are. Our hero doesn't know what will happen after taking the journey. They don't know the perils that await, but they know that what lies ahead is far greater than where they have been. A truly epic journey requires the hero to affiliate themselves with the warrior's spirit—to grow, to shed what does not serve them moving forward. They must face the darkness ahead of them and allow their fears to be tested so a new, courageous version of them can be born. Our hero searches for a path they're supposed to take, and soon realizes that the path their destiny is calling them to has not yet been paved. They must blaze their own trail in order to reach the greatness that is calling them. They face challenges, low valleys, triumphs, high mountains, and euphoric wins. In the end, they go home a hero because they had the courage to pursue their dream. One of my favorite sayings, by Antonio Machado, goes, "Traveler, there is no path. Paths are made by walking."

Our minds are good at rationalizing all kinds of excuses as to why we shouldn't blaze our own trails. But to listen to that rationalization and deny yourself that adventure is to deny yourself the life of your dreams. These fears are what are standing in your way between surviving life or truly living one. You mustn't allow your fears to dictate your destiny—and do not for a second think that a true hero isn't scared. If you're not scared, you're not not courageous—you're just not alive. Fear is good, and conquering that fear means you become really alive. What you desire is much more important than the fear that has consumed you.

Most of us live in fear and never pursue our big dreams because we're too afraid to leave the security of our old lives behind. But I'll tell you a secret that will change your life and dramatically shift your mentality if you apply it. Security is not about what you have; security is about how you think. When you take action consistently, you will conquer your fear and develop the courage it will take to live the adventure in your soul.

CHAPTER THIRTEEN:

The Wisdom of the Mountains and Cosmos

"When we try to pick out anything by itself, we find it hitched to everything else in the universe."
—*John Muir*

I. Mount Whitney

At 2:00 a.m., the alarm sounded. Instinctively, I slapped my blaring phone. I wasn't smacking my alarm out of dread and anxiety today though; I was smacking it out of pure adrenaline and excitement. I had been in and out of sleep for the last two hours waiting for it to go off anyway, anticipating the daring adventure that lay before us today—an adventure that at this point in my life, my brother and I deemed practically historic. I took a long breath and rolled over in my rock-hard bed in a discount motel in Lone Pine, California. The sun was a long way from coming up still. On the bed opposite me, I saw Marcus, eyes open.

"Ready?" he said.

"Ready," I answered.

Two hours of sleep isn't a lot, but on a morning with so much adrenaline and excitement coursing through my veins, it was all I needed for the trek in front of us. We checked out of our motel, started the engine of my car, and made the forty-five-minute drive to the where the true adventure would begin. Marcus and I had spent the last six months preparing and training for today, climbing the highest peaks in our local counties. We summited Orange County's Santiago Peak at 5,689 feet, then San Diego's Hot Springs Mountain at 6,535 feet, followed by Los Angeles's own Mount Baldy at 10,064 feet. Each hike was progressively higher and more intense to help us prepare for something we had in our hearts to do since learning in grade school that this mountain was not only the largest in all of California, but in the entire continental United States of America. On this day, we planned to climb and summit all 14,505 feet of the granddaddy of Californian peaks, Mount Whitney, a mountain so epic, grandiose, and stunningly beautiful that it is a part of the world-famous John Muir Trail. During our research of Mount Whitney, we discovered that most people summit the peak and return to the trailhead in two to three days. To this day, I don't know if it was Marcus's idea or mine, but we've always been the kind of brothers who push each other to be the best we can at any area of life, so we committed ourselves to climbing the tallest mountain in the continental United States in a single day. Perhaps it was a bit of youthful confidence and swagger that got us to make that decision, but I like to think it was the thrill of the challenge that was most alluring to us.

We pulled up to the trailhead and threw on our backpacks, they were light enough to not be a huge burden for us but packed enough to carry more than a day's worth of food and water if we needed it. We made our first step toward the peak that had been beckoning to us since grade school. The night was pitch-black—no city lights within dozens of miles here—but in the darkness, we found the trail relatively easily. The wilderness has always called to me, for in nature, I have always felt a certain sense of freedom as I am able to wander freely without societal impositions. Climbing through here, the feeling was stronger than ever. The initial switchbacks up the first hill took about an hour; the romance of the adventure carried us forward in good spirits, even with a severe lack of sleep. Who needed dreams when we were living one, right? At the top of the first peak, we carried on further, just enough until we could find a comfortable spot to sit and rest. Upon seeing a flat rock, we sat to briefly rest our bones while rejuvenating with some water. My phone, of course, had no reception deep within the Sierra Nevada mountains, but I had pulled up a random song from my phone library to listen to, hopefully to keep us excited. The song is one I'll not soon forget: "Breeze," by Australian multi-instrumentalist Xavier Rudd. We both lay down and gazed at the night sky as it reverberated through the wilderness before Mount Whitney.

Now, I have seen a lot of beautiful things in my life, but save for the northern lights in Iceland, I have never had an experience quite as stunning as lying in the Sierra Nevada forest, listening to this particular song on this particular night. As I looked up at the sky, I saw that the stars were illuminated brighter than I had ever seen them. Miles and miles away from any light pollution from the city allowed the true, unfiltered majesty of the stars to shine their brightest on our little resting spot.

As I was gazing up, these stars—around which thousands upon thousands of different planets orbited—captivated my imagination and filled my spirit. I felt connected to everything on a visceral level. I felt in my entire being—not that I was born from the universe, but rather that I was the universe manifesting itself as, well . . . me. I didn't see all those thousands upon thousands of stars and feel isolated, small, and insignificant. I saw those stars and felt connected to it all. I grew up loving everything there was about astronomy and cosmic law, so while I wasn't exactly a quantum physicist, I knew enough about science and the universe to have fun talking about it around the dinner table with Carl Sagan and Stephen Hawking. Coupled with this experience, what I understood about the universe touched me so deeply. I understood that the very atoms that formed life on Earth—our very beings and existences—came from the atoms that comprised all stars, including the stars that were shining brightly on this night. Molecules like nitrogen, oxygen, and carbon were not only the elements of these stars, but of life itself. The universe was within me, as me. These stars eventually perished and exploded their atoms all across the galaxy. Prior to this moment, I had felt like I was part of the universe—a bit lost and alone, but still part of this great cosmic arena. I felt like I lived in the universe. But on this night, with Xavier Rudd playing from my phone, my brother and I embarking on the greatest adventure of our lives up to that point, and lovingly gazing at the stars, I experienced the entire universe within me, a blissful solitude hidden among the deep stillness of the mountains. The mountains and cosmos seemed to divulge their secrets, and I was open to receiving them.

I had always felt small in the world. Lost and wandering through a great big world on an even bigger cosmic playground. Who was I to have any significance in the grand scheme of the universe? I was a "poor little me," as Alan Watts might say, living a meager existence in a nihilistic world. On this night, however, I felt as big as those stars that shined light-years upon light-years to make their way to my eyes. How could I not? What was within those stars was also within me. I felt connected to the Earth, to those stars, to everyone I knew, to my brother sitting beside me. So connected—more than ever. Watching that night sky, I felt alive, and big. I felt as big as the entire universe, because in a way, I was the entire universe. I felt like I had the entire universe all to myself and the entire universe had me all to itself. I think my brother saw me smiling at what I'm sure seemed like nothing in particular, but I also feel like he understood on some level too. *Life . . . is a grand gift*, I thought.

"We got a mountain to climb. Let's rock," my brother said. We stood, and without saying anything further, took our next steps toward Mount Whitney's peak.

As we continued to climb, the sun's rays began to peek over Sequoia National Park, which was a much-needed reprieve from the freezing cold at such a high altitude, even in the summer. Slowly, we made our way up a grueling part of the hike known as 99 switchbacks. This area of the climb is especially difficult because by the time you get to this point, you can see the entirety of Mount Whitney, but rather than climb straight up the face of the mountain, you must go around the side, walking back and forth, from side to side ninety-nine times, with the peak of the mountain almost taunting you every time you turn back to face it. A beautiful mountain, but during this prolonged stretch, it was more persistently haunting than anything else. At this time, Marcus's two hours of sleep began to show. The risk of getting altitude sickness is a repercussion of trying to summit the highest mountain in the contiguous United States in a single day and, coupled with his apparent exhaustion, that altitude sickness began to show, so we sat on the fresh snow to take another break in the sun, which didn't provide much comfort from the icy cold at this elevation.

"Want to turn back?" he asked.

A long pause. The beauty of a majestic early morning cosmic show was long fading. I didn't know how to answer. I was fading and fading fast. I thought of how insane it was to try to climb this mountain in a single day when everybody else was doing it in two or three. I was tired and my instinct was to turn around. After all, if we went back now, we could get back to a cheap motel by midnight, grab some comfort food, and share stories in the hot tub about how we would do it all again next year. My mind wandered, but my heart begged me to persevere.

Go home, Travis, my wolf of hate was screaming.

Koa, my wolf of love whispered.

"No. Let's keep going. We can do this. We need to," I answered. No words left in either of us, we jumped to our feet, as if we were both waiting for permission from ourselves and each other to continue. As always, one foot in front of the other, heading toward the looming but stunning face of our destination.

Time stretched on and on until 99 switchbacks was finally finished. Now it was time to scale the backside of the mountain. Icy climbs didn't make for confident footing and our climb slowed even further. The altitude sickness was getting worse in my brother and also starting to get to me. Becoming slowly delirious, as we were ill-prepared with enough water, we both began eating snow off the mountainside. I was dizzy, confused, and scared, but I knew that turning back would be harder, as reaching the summit would give us an emotional boost that would carry us back home—something to talk about on the journey back, at least. Though I knew we could reach the top of the mountain, I also knew it would be challenging. I was especially concerned for Marcus. His body looked tired, but he also looked like he needed the push, like he would regret it forever if we turned back. We pushed on.

After what seemed like days, but what, in reality, was no more than thirteen hours, we finally climbed our last steps onto the peak of the highest mountain in the continental United States. Fatigue, delirium, and pure exhaustion were not enough to keep us from staring in unbridled amazement at this view. Not only did the entire Sequoia National Park present itself before us, but so did cities upon cities, valleys upon valleys, and mountains upon mountains. Breathing in this mountain air, I felt—no, I *was*—on top of the entire world. Basking in nature's glory, the thrill of triumph overwhelmed me. Whether it was the pure delusion of altitude sickness or something more didn't matter to me, but in this moment, I cried tears of joy—not small tears, because I was openly weeping. The early morning experience of the stars combined with this view, which I never in my life thought I would reach, culminated in something far more than simply making it to the top of a mountain. I saw a new perspective on the fragility of life. I saw my life's problems and challenges down there, not up here with me. They didn't have to be here with me. From this vantage point, I saw that I was only carrying them because I thought I had to. It wasn't what I was carrying in my life that burdened me down; it was how I was choosing to carry it. Everything I identified as myself was down there; but my true self was up here, and it was completely free. Yes, I survived the climb, but for the first time since I was a child, I was truly alive. I raised my arms to the sky and hugged my brother closer than I ever remembered.

"We did it, bro."

When climbing a mountain, you are often faced with low and dark valleys, incredibly challenging obstacles, and steep, seemingly insurmountable slopes—much like life itself. But every single step of the journey, if you are persistent, gets you closer to your peak, and every single peak is well within reach if you just keep on moving. Standing at the summit, we had no reason to be there, other than to have an experience of life. I thought of the famous English mountaineer, George Mallory, who, when asked, "Why did you want to climb Mount Everest?" replied, curtly, "Because it's there."

II. *The Overview Effect*

Standing on top of a mountain changes a man's perspective of the world, and I can attest to this. If we allow ourselves to take in the beauty from such a high vantage point and get lost in the moment of awe, we will see less of ourselves and quickly forget our petty problems and feuds. We will see more of the world and, ultimately, our places in it. Sure, standing on top of a mountain looking down can change your perspective—but what would happen if you were standing on top of the world?

In 1971, astronaut Edgar Mitchell became the sixth man to walk on the moon. On the return journey, Mitchell would regularly look out of the window of his shuttle and gaze upon our home, Earth. He would take in the full majesty of it, watching it delicately float in the black and endless vastness of space. For this man who saw our planet from such a different perspective, the pure visual beauty of it was only the beginning. More than a visual connection, Edgar Mitchell was experiencing something emotional as well. A feeling of timelessness and pure euphoria simply overwhelmed him, as well as a feeling he claimed to be profoundly spiritual. He described waking up to the concept that each of his atoms were connected not only to the planet Earth, but also to every other person, animal, and atom in the entire universe. There was a feeling of ecstasy and a sense of being one with the cosmos and everything in it.

Many other astronauts have reported having a similar experience, including Yuri Gagarin, the first human being put into orbit around the Earth in 1961, and Rusty Schweickart, who performed testing on the lunar-landing systems of the Apollo 9 flight. The experience has become so widespread among those who travel in space that it has become known as the "overview effect." This term refers to the perspective shift of seeing the Earth firsthand in space, where national boundary lines disappear and conflicts between people and countries become less important. This experience often produces a noticeable change in attitude in these astronauts, as they understand the responsibility of this thing called life and the relationship between themselves and the rest of the world.

Andrew Newberg, a neuroscientist and co-founder of the Overview Institute has spent years studying how to identify someone who experienced space travel and the overview effect. He states that "there is a change in someone who has traveled to the outside of our planet," and his research is looking for answers as to why this occurs. This experience describes not a feeling of distance from the universe when gazing upon the Earth, but rather a sense of oneness with it—a sense that every fiber, cell, and molecule in the traveler's body is not separate, but instead connected to the entire universe. As astronauts who have studied astronomy and cosmology, they know the science of human connection to the universe—how the properties of exploding and dying stars change to form new planets, asteroids, and life. But reading about these concepts is one thing; they had never felt the emotional and physical connection of that concept before. A simple view of our planet from the outside looking in gave this to them.

Aside from the overwhelming feeling of connection to the universe gained by seeing the Earth from such a distance, these astronauts also gained an incredible perspective of the fragility of our home and life itself. The overview of our Earth allows those who are fortunate enough to witness it to see our home as a planet with no borders, and perspective allows them to see the pettiness of baseless fear, the absurdity of wars among ourselves, and the sheer pettiness of feuding itself. From a cosmic perspective, life is not viewed as something to be simply survived, but something to be lived. And the Earth is seen as a living, breathing organism that should be taken care of. While floating over Europe and Africa, seeing no borders or separate people, could you imagine the silliness of not pursuing the life you desire? Can you imagine seeing such a beautiful home in all its glory, and knowing that its citizens go through life worrying about what might happen if they just go for it? After all, from this kind of vantage point, you can see that you are here for a fraction of a fraction of a fraction of a blip in the grand scheme of the universe, taking a fleeting ride in a meat-coated skeleton made from stardust, riding on a rock that is hurling at 67,000 miles per hour through a massive solar system, which is only one of billions of solar systems in billions of galaxies in a boundless cosmic arena. So, what were you scared of again?

This phenomenon allows us to humble ourselves, to see the population of our planet not as many separate races and cultures, but as only one race. The thing is, as much as we would love to travel Earth's orbit and experience the overview effect personally, we don't have to have that experience to understand what it means for us and our lives. We can see how delicate our tiny home and how fragile our existence is in the vastness of space and time, and begin to shift our attitudes and behaviors into living life the way we dream of it, and nurturing one another as fellow inhabitants of the same planet. The message is clear: be humble, be good, take care of our world, and be bold in life.

On top of a mountain, we may get a humbling perspective of our own lives; but on top of the world, we get a perspective of life itself.

III. Stamps on a Passport

Stamps on a passport are hardly the definition of a person, but to me, they can sometimes be a small indication of the kind of life a person has lived and a sampling of the attitude a person has about the world. To me, each stamp in that book is not just an ink marker necessary to pass through customs, but it is something much more meaningful—a story that should be told over a hot cup of coffee at a distant airport bar as the morning's first rays of light shimmer through the terminal windows. A passport can be a memoir of romance and adventure, one that probably includes as many memorable far-off encounters as missed and canceled flights. And even more than this, to me a stamp in a passport always represents a clearer understanding of home, our home. Not just our home country, but the planet Earth and the people who live on it.

Perhaps a single page in a traveler's passport tells the story of a great adventure through the Amazon rainforest, or another day spent traversing the bazaars of India. Maybe that stamp earned in Asia comes with a story about dining on live octopus in the heart of Tokyo! As I sit in airport bars around the world, often drinking the local specialty, I dig into my bag, pull out my own passport, and reflect on it with a smile and a little bit of pride. Each of the stamps I've earned fills me with nostalgia, of surf trips to Nicaragua, or the romance of celebrating St. Patrick's Day with the Irish in Dublin. But most of all, I gain perspective. The more my passport fills, the more my mind opens, and the more I feel how big this world is and how insignificantly small I am as a result, and ironically also how connected I am to the whole thing, how connected we all are to one another.

No matter how different we may think we all are, how "stupid" we may think those in opposing political parties are, how backward we may think the remote tribes in Africa or the Amazon are, how strange the cultures that play that "weird" game called goat hockey in the Far East may seem to us, good travel teaches us that we're all just different facets of the same tribe. One family, one group of people on the same rock in space, traveling around the same star that each and every one of us get to see rise and set every day; looking up at the same set of constellations every single night. We are all wondering just how meaningful we are on this planet, within this vast galaxy, this unfathomably large expanse of the universe where we all reside and that all six billion of us call home. Even remote tribes share and understand the meaning behind a smile, and they have desires to be loved and appreciated. The people of Afghanistan enjoy their goat hockey as much as we enjoy our football! We are really not so different. Travel—not vacation—has offered me the experience of not only discovering the world, but myself as well. Filling up my passport over the years has taught me humbling and profound lessons. We are all really in this game of life searching for the same things—some happiness and just a bit of meaning.

Getting a stamp on our passports is far more than just going on a trip, if we're doing it right. Stepping off that plane and onto unfamiliar soil is only the beginning of something remarkably life-changing, if we only allow our minds and hearts to be as open as our eyes (and wallets) during our stays.

Taking the opportunity to get a bit uncomfortable and explore the experiences and people that a new place has to offer will likely challenge your preconceived notions about a place and its people, and can offer new insight into your own home, even though your own home might be thousands of miles away. Sitting at a bar in Chile, enjoying a beer and telling jokes with the local sitting next to you might help you understand that, while the people of South America have unique and interesting customs, when it comes down to a human level, they aren't so different from you after all. Knowing that we're not so differ-ent from one another, how could you return home and treat those who are different from you? Walking through the slums of Thailand will offer a sobering reality check and show you that all the complaining you're doing back home, about how hard life can be, is nothing compared to what these people are suffering. When you return home after seeing this, wouldn't you value what you already have in your life?

Exploration in exotic lands, connecting with strangers around the globe, getting out of your comfort zone in strange places, climbing mountains and seeing a new perspective of the Earth, not only means discovery on the map, but also within yourself. To travel well is to understand the world and the citizens of Earth even better. To travel well means to come back every time a bit humbler and with a greater understanding of who you really are.

CHAPTER FOURTEEN:

Embracing the Traveler's Code

"Do not go where the path may lead, go instead where there is no path and leave a trail."
—*Muriel Strode*

I. New Zealand

It had always been a dream of mine, once I finally became a coach full time, to live in another country for an extended period of time. While working on my own purpose, I got to the point where I was able to create my own schedule and work with my clients from anywhere in the world, and I wanted to more boldly step into that possibility. While I had seen some beautiful places in the world, I had only visited these places. What I really wanted to do was to stay somewhere foreign and really get involved in another culture. When Jessica and I met, she moved to the United States for a year so we could be together. When that year was over, she asked how I felt about going to live in Australia for a while. Without any hesitation, I sai yes and we booked our tickets.

The thing I immediately noticed about living in Australia is that everything seems like it will kill you. As my new Aussie barber explained it to me, "Mate, if it looks like it'll kill ya, it'll kill ya. If it looks like it won't kill ya, it'll still probably kill ya!" This kind of realization—that anything can send you six feet under at any moment—leads to a state of subtle anxiety that some violent and untimely death is perpetually just around the corner. Once we became as comfortable and settled in as we could be in Australia, Jessica and I booked a couple of plane tickets overseas and across the border, to the country's southeast neighbor, the land of the long white cloud—New Zealand. The plan was to rent a car in Auckland, at the top of the North Island, and road trip all the way down to Milford Sound in the South Island. I never had the opportunity to go on a cross-country American road trip, so I was fired up to go on an honest-to-goodness, cross-country Kiwi adventure. New Zealand was always on my radar, and the fact that it's widely considered the adventure capital of the world certainly helped pique my interest.

As we hit the road out of Auckland, the beauty of the surrounding countryside immediately struck me. Since I knew this was where *The Lord of the Rings* was filmed, the farmland filled with lush, rolling hills captured my imagination as a place you might actually find a hobbit living in. It really did feel straight out of Middle Earth, especially when our new Kiwi friend Andy told me that it's socially acceptable to walk around barefoot all the time. *This*, I thought, *is my kind of place*. I made a pact with myself and my new friend, Andy, that on this two-week Kiwi adventure, I would embrace my inner hobbit and not wear shoes. The highlight of the North Island was kayaking to an isolated and sheltered island in the ocean called Whenuakura, otherwise known to the locals as Donut Island (so named because it's actually a dormant old volcano crater that resembles a donut). Over the years, erosion has created a small tunnel about thirty feet wide that can luckily be used to kayak into the middle of the crater, which reveals a lush green forest with inviting, blue swimming water in the center. We spent all afternoon swimming in the warm ocean water, hiking barefoot through the greenery, doing some of the highest and scariest cliff jumps of my life, and smiling so much it began to hurt our faces.

The following day, we trekked down to the world-famous surf spot Raglan. From my campsite in the morning and early afternoon, I caught up and worked with some of my clients online, and then later hit the surf, crossing another item off my bucket list by surfing the longest-breaking left wave in the entire Southern Hemisphere—something I had wanted to do since I was a kid, since I'd seen it featured in the classic 1966 surf film, *The Endless Summer*. That is one day I'll never forget—getting to do what I really love, having powerful, life-changing coaching conversations with extraordinary people, engaging in my purpose, and getting to surf a wave like Raglan. After the surf, I walked back to our campsite and made friends with some curious cows. When you're walking through lush green hills, still wet and salty from an incredible surf, and then ten cows walk up to you wanting to be petted, you realize, "Holy crap, I'm in New Zealand!"

If traveling by car on the way from the North Island to the south, you begin to notice how the already stunning and majestic landscapes become gradually more dramatic and breathtaking the further south you go. As lush, green hills slowly gave way to epic, towering mountains, we pulled off the side of the road just to look at and take it all in. We wandered off the beaten path often—once into beautiful hot springs just begging to be relaxed in and enjoyed. Laying our heads in the springs for a bit, feeling the warm rain drops trickling off the trees, and immersing ourselves in the hot steam of the creek, I couldn't help but reflect on Ray Bradbury's famous words: "Stuff your eyes with wonder, live as if you'd drop dead in ten seconds. See the world. It's more fantastic than any dream made or paid for in factories."

After ten days of driving south through the country, we made it to our final destination, the world-famous Milford Sound. English poet Rudyard Kipling called this place "the eighth wonder of the world." Upon stepping barefoot onto the rocky sand, being greeted by a wide-open inlet of dark ocean water and surrounded by all sides with soaring mountainscapes and behemoth, cascading waterfalls, his sentiments quickly became my own. You are instantly consumed by the beauty and majesty of it all. The cliffs lift all the way from the dark ocean, stretching into the sky and rising past the clouds. *If Mother Nature were an artist*, I thought, *Milford Sound would most certainly be her masterpiece.*

As I stood, dwarfed among the skyscraping fjords, remarking on the raw beauty that this world has offered me and that seemed to culminate in this dramatic and powerful setting, I also thought of my life story leading up to that point. I took a step back mentally and thought of where I had journeyed to get to this point. I reflected on everything it took to get me here at this very moment in time. I thought about all the challenges, all the aimless wandering, all the false starts and failures. I thought of all the adventures and stories, all the naysayers and supporters. I thought of all the incredible highs and all the difficult lows. I reflected on all of it and here I was at this moment, a man on purpose, living with purpose. I laughed as I realized that I was really living my life on my terms—living my lifelong dream to be free and to be able to do what I truly love with my life. From miserably sitting in my Volkswagen van on the 405 Freeway—lost and aimlessly wandering through life—to standing joyously in Milford Sound, found and purposefully wandering, I felt gratitude for my adventure of life and was proud of the man I had become. Was it challenging at times? Yes. Was it worth it? I thought, *Of course. Every single step of the way.*

Here I was: standing tall among Mother Nature's masterpiece, having embarked on the adventure of a lifetime, living my purpose of a lifetime.

II. Getting Lucky

The adventure of purpose does not take itself—you must take it. The message within this book alone will never change your life for you, just as the knowledge I've gained on my brief time here on Earth hasn't gone out of its way to guide me. Many of us have the idea that when we buy a book, that once we finish it, it will be like some magic pill that will make our lives better—take it once, do nothing, and expect the results to show themselves. We put the book back on the bookshelf without applying any of it to our lives but expecting results anyway. The wisdom sits in our bookshelves, collects dust, and its teachings are quickly forgotten about. Self-discovery and growth will never take the journey for you, just like a trip to another country will never make its path to you; you must take the steps yourself. The message will only provide you with the tools so that you can embark on your own quest. This is the profound beauty of the adventure: it is your journey to make. The journey itself will often require you to dig deep, to get out of your comfort zone, work hard, and apply the spirit of these lessons to your life. When you do this, your life will grow dramatically. Life itself is not something that happens to you; life is what you make it. One of the most uplifting facts about life is a simple one: You get to create your own! You get to take all those incredible aspirations, visions, and dreams for yourself and turn them into your reality. You hold the power to design your life; nobody else has that power, not unless you give it to them. We mustn't let life and all the obstacles that come with it master us; rather we should be vigilant in taking back our power and forming it into what we aspire to be. An extraordinary life doesn't just happen by accident—it has to be designed and created. It's easy to submit to the forces of whatever happens to us, thinking that if there were any opportunity for a great life, it would just present itself on its own, on some random day in the future.

Begin building your map. How can you make it to the life of your dreams? What small steps can you start taking now? What will you have to do to get to that point that you dream of? Journey toward your outcome, always moving toward that dream life, never staying still and certainly never moving backward. The great things in life won't ever happen to you; you have to put yourself out there by working toward your destination.

You don't have to wait for a winning lottery ticket to do what you really love and fulfill those long-held dreams of yours. You don't have to wait until retirement to finally live the life you've always dreamed of. Millions of people are waiting for that metaphorical golden ticket, waiting to punch out of their jobs for the last time and finally start living, doing what their hearts are calling them toward. They're waiting—indefinitely waiting. Continually standing by for some good fortune, that "right time," or some ideal situation to occur so they can start living life. But that wait comes at the greatest price of all—existing unfulfilled, putting things off until a "better time," and in the end of our days, looking back at this one shot at life and asking, "What if I would have really lived my life with passion?"

An exceedingly large number of people wait so long to live that those dreams will remain nothing more than that—dreams.

Because they waited too long. You don't have to settle for any less than what you truly desire, what makes you come alive. You must stop waiting and start doing.

I could've gone the easy route plenty of times throughout my life. I could have easily found a million ways to talk myself out of pursuing my purpose, because a million times I was just "not ready yet." I knew I was scared, but I embraced the adventure because I wanted to open myself up to purpose, to live and not to wait. I committed to getting my feet wet before I could talk myself out of doing it again. This, in my opinion, is the truest and most honest spirit of adventure: if you know it's good for you, if you know it's your calling, if you know it's in your heart, if you know, you take the leap and ask questions as you go.

By taking step after step, you will make things happen for yourself. You must lean into your purpose. You don't have to jump right into it, but you need to put your feet in the water and explore the possibilities, uncovering more clues and paths as you move along. If you love the idea of training dolphins, do something as small as researching it, swimming in the ocean more often, or talking to others who have already trained dolphins. If you want to hike more often, your odds of going on hikes greatly improve if you spend time with others who enjoy the same thing. The more you surround yourself with others who share your interests, the more you learn about the things you want to do, and the more likely it is that you will start doing things that will make them happen. Don't wait to live—live today. Your life literally depends on it. You will never survive the running of the bulls if you don't go running with the bulls!

You know those types of people who always seem to have the best luck at whatever they do in life—maybe they found some great new job, or happened to be in the right place at the right time and received some beautiful opportunity that you missed out on. They go through life with what appears to be a series of happy accidents. Others have it not-so-great—they work hard every day at the same soul-crushing, low-paying job and seem to miss every opportunity by this much. They are waiting for some proverbial knight in shining armor or magical change in circumstances. The difference in these people isn't any kind of luck at all, though; it's perspective—the ones with the "lucky" lives are busy doing things while the ones who sit jealous on the sidelines are busy waiting for things.

I had an old childhood friend once who bought a new bike after working most of the summer for it. I distinctly recall all the other kids on my street talking about how "lucky" he was to have such a great new bicycle, and they were seriously jealous of how "fortunate" he was. How did things work out so well for him that he ended up with the coolest bike in town? It wasn't luck at all. He put a plan in place and worked hard for months to provide his own opportunities. He wasn't lucky in the slightest—he had created the luck himself. Having a Guinness once in Ireland, I talked with a local Dubliner at the oldest pub in Europe. We talked about Irish luck. "The harder you work, the luckier you get, lad," he said. I took that kind of Irish wisdom to the bank.

What are you willing to sacrifice to achieve your goals? In order to pursue the life that you want, you must give up the comfortable habits that have done you no good up until this point. Sacrifice your time, money, and energy *now* so that your future self will be able to reap the rewards of the changes you brought into your life. If you invest your time and energy (and money) into learning now, you will be able to create those "lucky" opportunities years from now. If you want something you have never had before, then you have to be willing to do something that you have never done before.

Everything that you want requires a surrender of something on your part—time, energy, or money. If dreams were free, everyone would have attained them. If you want your life to improve and bring more exciting opportunities your way, then you have to try new things and embrace the experience. If you keep doing things the same way, then they are going to continue exactly as they are. Change is immensely more powerful than chance. Chance is for people who wish; change is for people who accomplish.

Along your journey, through your highs and lows, you will discover some adversity. Society is built in a way that embraces working hard for money over personal fulfillment. Frankly, the greater your vision, the harder it is to live an authentic life without being ridiculed. From practically the moment we come out of the womb, those who are already here condition us with their ways of seeing the world. They educate us on how they think a person should live; we are defined by their terms of success. They say these rules help us become an upstanding member of society, but all it really seems to do is tame our inner wild things and cage us into their way of life. This can be incredibly challenging for anyone embarking on their adventure of purpose, but every challenge we ever face is a call to a great adventure.

We are to go through life, working so hard to become "successful" and "important." We are to listen to the rules given to us and follow them exactly. We are to become what our parents want us to be, and when we finally reach the point in our lives and careers where we've "made it," why, then, do we feel so much internal conflict? We do our best to fit in and to make it in life, but our inner spirits slowly become shattered, and our childhood sense of self is destroyed because we've spent our whole lives living someone else's expectation of who we should be instead of being totally authentic to who we are.

This is always the point in life when we wake up in a cold sweat, and when we crave emotional support from outsiders who can tell us we're doing a good job at the life we hate. We think it will help ease the internal pain, but the core issue has not been resolved: we are not listening to our inner compasses. We seek validation from those who aren't who we want to be so that we can feel better about ourselves in a place we don't want to be. I hope you see the vicious circle.

You are looking for validation that what you seek to do is important. This is normal behavior; it's part of being human. It's completely natural to look for validation; after all, we are a social species, and validation makes us feel pretty good; it lifts us up, even inspires us. But as we take our first steps on our journeys of purpose, we will often break some of the expectations of our society, so the challenge is that validations may be few and far between, especially in the beginning.

To truly embrace the traveler's code is to be a little quirky, to own your weird, but most importantly, to be "you"—even if that means going against the world's expectation of who you should be—and to make no apologies about it. We will do things that the world may not understand—and that's a good thing. You must understand that extraordinary things were never done by remaining ordinary. Living a life of purpose comes with living in a way that is purely authentic to you. If you're living in a way that the world expects you to, I'm willing to bet that you are not completely authentic to who you are. To live your journey of purpose, you must learn to become indifferent to the opinions of others. The magic is, the less you look for others' approval, the more of it they'll eventually give you. People may say "you've changed," like it's a bad thing, but that's like mourning for a cocoon after a butterfly has emerged.

I pursued what I believed in so much that many people around me thought I was absolutely nuts. At first, I was told that there wasn't an audience for what I wanted to do, and then when I found my audience, I was told there was no money in what I wanted to do, and it goes on and on. I spent a big chunk of my life traveling in a different direction than everyone else around me. I had no validation from others, and I was ridiculed. The funny and ironic thing is that those very same people who ridiculed me are now asking if I'm hiring. It's interesting how the impossible suddenly becomes possible in others' minds once it's been done. Through my journey, I learned that "impossible" is just another way to say, "I don't know how." I learned that being my authentic self would let my true friends make themselves known to me, and those who were not truly friends would fade away. This isn't a sad thing; this is a beautiful thing. It helps to trim what has not served you in your life.

People, especially those who are close to you, may not fully understand you. They will likely question you; they will talk about you behind your back; and they will call you crazy (like it's a bad thing!). You don't need their support or validation, though. Be like the traveler going their own way on their own path. Be all right if they don't understand you. You don't need to convince anyone to see things your way—just learn to accept that they don't get it, and choose to love them anyway. Part of my motivation in working toward my own dreams was to prove my naysayers wrong and to show them that dreams do come true if you commit to working for those dreams. They see it now.

III. The Law of Association

Motivational speaker Jim Rohn once observed, "You are the average of the five people you spend the most time with." I wholly agree with this sentiment. We tend to see successful people spending most of their time with other successful people. We generally see fit people hanging out with other people who are fit. How many times can you recall a group of positive, happy people having a negative pessimist in their ranks? Birds of a feather flock together.

It doesn't matter where you grew up or what kind of grades you got in school. It doesn't really matter what skills you have today. What matters the most to the person you want to be in the future is who you choose to associate yourself with . . . and who you choose to disassociate yourself with.

There may be some people in your life who make you feel drained after only an hour with them, yet you spend as much or more than a few days a week with them. There may be other people in your life who make you feel absolutely rejuvenated after time with them, yet you only see them during brief and off-the-cuff moments. This is not a fault of yours. Most people don't go through their day-to-day life thinking about their toxic or potentially positive relationships. Your relationships build you, though. They help build your dreams, your happiness, and your overall quality of life. However, they can also build your nightmares, your sadness, and the overall feeling of helplessness in your life.

Can you imagine trying to live your purpose when you have friends and family around you who are always ridiculing rather than supporting you? If you hang around negative people constantly, it's beyond unlikely that you will ever have a positive approach to life. This goes both ways. If you hang around positive people consistently, it's unlikely that you will develop a negative approach to life.

It's important to spend some time evaluating the people whom you spend the most time with. I'm sure there will be coworkers, family, and other friends on this list. Think about each person. Do they push you forward in life in one way or another, or do they push you backward? Do they motivate and inspire you, or do they only contribute to crushing your dreams? Do they make you smile when you're with them, or do they make you sad? Decide who on this list you want to spend less time with and start pursuing actions that will cut your time with them. On that same list, write down the names of people you want to spend more time with. Start pursuing actions that will increase your time with them. At the end of the list, who do you have left? What would your life look like if you were the average of these five people?

IV. A Single Step

You must quit trying to please everyone; it will never happen, nor should it. If you try to please everyone in the world, you will please no one. Embrace who you authentically are, embrace nonconformity, and embrace the traveler's code. Like leaping out of your comfort zone, you must learn to get comfortable without other people understanding your journey, because the only benefit of conforming is that everyone likes you except you.

If you listen to what everyone is telling you that you should be doing, you run the risk of actually getting stuck in that thing. Usually those who are the loudest proponents of working a soul-crushing job are those who already dread going to work, those whose lives seem to be an endless cycle of hitting the snooze button, crawling miserably out of bed, driving to a job they loathe, and going through the motions at work just to pay the bills. This sounds like insanity, right? Who are these people who are so dissatisfied with their lives that they tell you what to do with yours? I've met too many people who worked so hard to have tons of money at any cost, and when they finally achieved financial wealth, they then realized that even seven figures wasn't worth a lifetime of unhappiness and misery.

So many kids are raised to believe that when they grow up, their future jobs have to inevitably be boring and soul-crushing, and that only a select, lucky few get to do something they really love. The rest of us have to settle for a job that pays the bills, working to support other people's businesses and dreams—living out of alignment with our core values so we can help other people live in alignment with theirs. But a bright future of work you love is not about luck—it's about persistence. It may seem like a secret to some, but you can do something about it. We've too easily fallen into this hoax that work is only something to do to make money. You are not stuck. If you're just coming out of high school or college and have no idea what you want to do, that's okay. Even if you've been at this dreaded job your whole life, it's never too late to get out there and start living your purpose. Wouldn't it be incredible to actually get out of bed every morning with a smile on your face, looking forward to the day ahead—to be excited about a life you love? Wouldn't it be a life worth living if you could earn money doing what you love? Anyone can find a way to do what they love if they make the effort to pursue it; and if other people are doing it, that means you can, too. A dream job isn't something hidden away that is almost impossible to attain. It's actually pretty easy to get; you only have to open your mind and want it bad enough.

Don't allow yourself to settle for hating your life for forty hours a week and dreading that job for the rest of the time that you have off. Don't allow yourself to follow the pre-paved trail because it's what everyone else seems to be doing; don't resist dealing with the discomfort and become nothing more than a reaction to the demands of the world. Once you begin the journey toward the life of your dreams, you'll feel good about even the smallest progress made. Growth in this field may be slow to begin with, but over time you will notice your advancement, like that of a snowball rolling down a mountain, gaining speed and volume as it moves along its path—once you get started, it will be hard to stop you! Give yourself the gift of a great career that you get excited about and actually look forward to every day, and you will live a life of purpose and nothing less.

Spending your life as anyone other than who you are is absolute lunacy. Following your true north is an adventure; it's a quest for fulfillment over stagnancy; it's a journey of self-discovery over living other people's expectations of who you should be. The traveler's code is to understand that it takes an unconventional spirit to do extraordinary things, to engage in pursuing something meaningful, and to live a life worth writing about; it's understanding that life is too short to wait for a special occasion to live—that life itself is a special occasion! When you find your true north and follow your inner compass, when you choose to embark on the adventure of purpose, you will not only find meaning in the destination, but also in your very first steps. You will discover parts of you that you never knew existed. Your heart will sing even more loudly than before, and you will start to listen even more closely.

The greatest adventure of your life begins with a single step.

Are you ready?

REFERENCES

U.K. Health and Safety Executive. 2019. "Work-related stress, anxiety or depression statistics in Great Britain." Annual statistics. https://www.hse.gov.uk/statistics/causedis/stress.pdf

U.S. Census Bureau (Americans at Age 31: Labor Market Activity, Education and Partner Status Summary, 2018)

Toshimasa Sone, OTR, BA, Naoki Nakaya, PhD, Kaori Ohmori, MD, PhD, Taichi Shimazu, MD, PhD, Mizuka Higashiguchi, PhD, Masako Kakizaki, MS, Nobutaka Kikuchi, MD, PhD, Shinichi Kuriyama, MD, PhD, And Ichiro Tsuji, MD, PhD (Sense of Life Worth Living (Ikigai) and Mortality in Japan: Ohsaki Study, 1994)

David B. Yaden, Jonathan Iwry, Kelley J. Slack, Johannes C. Eiechstaedt, Yukun Zhao, George E. Vaillant, Andrew B. Newberg. (The overview effect: Awe and self-transcendent experience in space flight. Psychology of Consciousness: Theory, Research, and Practice, 2016)

GRAND PATRONS

Chantal Secours
Clay Loveless
Gabriel Barton
Jaimie Hamlin
Jodie Matthews
Kariea Simmons
Lizzi Whaley
Marie Ann Labbee
Maurice Martineau
Mikael Lund
Timothy Barton

INKSHARES

INKSHARES is a reader-driven publisher and producer based in Oakland, California. Our books are selected not by a group of editors, but by readers worldwide.

While we've published books by established writers like *Big Fish* author Daniel Wallace and *Star Wars: Rogue One* scribe Gary Whitta, our aim remains surfacing and developing the new author voices of tomorrow.

Previously unknown Inkshares authors have received starred reviews and been featured in the *New York Times*. Their books are on the front tables of Barnes & Noble and hundreds of independents nationwide, and many have been licensed by publishers in other major markets. They are also being adapted by Oscar-winning screenwriters at the biggest studios and networks.

Interested in making your own story a reality? Visit Inkshares.com to start your own project or find other great books.

Printed in the USA
CPSIA information can be obtained
at www.ICGtesting.com
JSHW082200140824
68134JS00014B/350